BLACK
PRIVILEGE
PUBLISHING
ATRIA

ALABAMA STATE WAS THE PLACE. PSYCHOLOGY WAS MY PASSION. I NEEDED TO FIND A PLUG. TO STAY WITHIN MY OWN FREQUENCY. I WAS DIFFERENT FROM MOST. I WAS MORE GIFTED THAN MOST. THEM COPS WOULD CRASH OUR CRIB. NOT MOVING WAS ACTUALLY A MOVE. EVERYTHING HAPPENS FOR A REASON. LOYALTY IS FOUNDATION. TO PASS ON THE DEAL.

THE VOICE IN MY HEAD IS GOD

2 CHAINZ

with Derrick Harriell

BLACK PRIVILEGE PUBLISHING

ATRIA

New York Amsterdam/Antwerp London
Toronto Sydney/Melbourne New Delhi

ATRIA
An Imprint of Simon & Schuster, LLC
1230 Avenue of the Americas
New York, NY 10020

First Black Privilege Publishing/Atria Books hardcover edition March 2026

BLACK PRIVILEGE PUBLISHING/ATRIA BOOKS and colophon are registered trademarks of Simon & Schuster, LLC

Simon & Schuster strongly believes in freedom of expression and stands against censorship in all its forms. For more information, visit BooksBelong.com.

For information about special discounts for bulk purchases, please contact Simon & Schuster Special Sales at 1-866-506-1949 or business@simonandschuster.com.

The Simon & Schuster Speakers Bureau can bring authors to your live event. For more information or to book an event, contact the Simon & Schuster Speakers Bureau at 1-866-248-3049 or visit our website at www.simonspeakers.com.

Interior design by Davina Mock-Maniscalco

Manufactured in the United States of America

3 5 7 9 10 8 6 4

Library of Congress Control Number has been applied for.

ISBN 978-1-6680-3115-5
ISBN 978-1-6680-3117-9 (ebook)

Dedicated to Pops

If you wrote a autobiography, you'd have to sue yourself.
Yo' lying ass.

—"Where U Been"

CONTENTS

CONTENTS

PREFACE

LIKE WI-FI (I'M CONNECTED)

I want to introduce you to the secrets of my success. How my consciousness led to my success. The voice in my head. This is nothing tangible or topical, a lot like love. You only can feel these things.

In this book, I will try and teach you how to feel what you already have inside of you. How to just shut up and listen to the inner voice. I will teach you to think clearly. To be confident about the decisions you make, based on the nudges you get.

After reading this book I hope that you will become a better person. I hope that you will become a better decision-maker. I hope that you will become more confident in everything you do.

After you read this book, you'll be more tapped in. You'll be more resourceful. You'll be confident in the outfit you put on. This book will help you get through your uncertainties. This book will qualify you in listening more to your heart.

This is a self-help reading. Well, maybe this isn't a self-help book, but sometimes you got to help yourself. When people say "I felt something in my spirit," sometimes you need to listen. A part of helping yourself is learning how to listen to the voice in your head.

I'm sure you've had conversations with people who've casually used the phrase "something told me" to describe experiences they wish they had avoided. They might've said something like, "Something told me not to go on that date," or "Something told me not to eat dinner at that restaurant," or "Something told me not to take that new job," or "Something told me not to buy that car from that bootleg dealership."

Sometimes people use the phrase to describe something good that's happened. "Something told me to go to that party, and that's where I ended up meeting my wife," or "Something told me to invest in that stock," or "Something told me to go back to school and major in finance," or "I would've been in that traffic jam, but something told me to take the long way home." Man, I've listened to people say something told them not to do something, or to do something, too many times to count. I've actually said it myself a million times. Have you ever wondered just what that "something" is? That thing we feel inside but don't know how to talk about? This is one of the questions we're here to explore. What is that "something"?

Welcome to *The Voice In My Head Is God*. I'm hoping, wishing, and praying that after reading this book, you'll come out better than you came in. This has been a lifetime journey full of strategies and theories of mine.

I wanted to make a book that could affect something, change someone's life. As a rapper, I've always wanted to do a book. I've seen other rappers do books. I've even read some of them. I must say I've been impressed. But I'm different, so I wanted my content to be different yet personal. I know sometimes when I think of artists and their stories, a lot of it deals with the struggle. We all have struggles, and we all have stories to tell. But this book is not about out-struggling or out-traumatizing the next rapper. I'm tapped into a higher source. I'm Wi-Fi connected to a higher power. I'm trying to enlighten. I'm trying to draw some jewels. I'm trying to give you some game.

—Toni
February 1, 2025,
Atlanta, Georgia

OLD ME
Y MOM COULD RAISE A MAN.
OMETHING
OLD ME
O ENJOY THE RIDE.
GOD IS
LOVE.
SOMETHIN
TOLD M
GOD WAS INSIDE MY HEA
SOMETHIN
TOLD M
EVERYTHING HAPPEN
FOR A REASON.

SOMETHING TOLD ME

Something told me to put the money in my sock.
Something told me it was too good to be true.
Something told me to make the left turn.
Something told me to pass on that vacation.
Something told me women are born superheroes.
Something told me my mom could raise a man.
Something told me my mom knew things.
Something told me not to take all that weed to school.
Something told me my wife sensed something.
Something told me women are born intuitive.
Something told me not to borrow another nigga's scale.
Something told me that scale had bad juju.
Something told me a red Polo can get you caught.
Something told me not to trust the law.
Something told me Alabama State was the place.
Something told me psychology was my passion.
Something told me I needed to find a plug.
Something told me to stay within my own frequency.
Something told me I was different from most.
Something told me I was more gifted than most.
Something told me them cops would crash our crib.
Something told me not moving was actually a move.
Something told me everything happens for a reason.

Something told me loyalty is foundation.
Something told me to pass on the deal.
Something told me to understand the music game.
Something told me I needed to get out of my deal.
Something told me to understand my value.
Something told me to call it "Based on a T.R.U. Story."
Something told me I'd figure it out on the fly.
Something told me I was molded by the South Side.
Something told me real legends don't die.
Something told me 2 Chainz would become legendary.
Something told me my name is my brand.
Something told me I needed my own studio.
Something told me never wait on nobody.
Something told me Old National was natural.
Something told me to stop trapping cold turkey.
Something told me to watch the company I kept.
Something told me to keep God first.
Something told me God was inside my head.
Something told me God is love.
Something told me to keep my pops close.
Something told me to "Do it big."
Something told me the Cali wind was too still.
Something told me to invest what I make.
Something told me to connect with a young lady I'd just met.
Something told me to know the heartbeat of the people.
Something told me to always be the real me.
Something told me that eyes were on me.
Something told me to wear the Balenciaga.
Something told me to wear Bottega.
Something told me to wear Rick Owens.
Something told me to wear both chains.
Something told me my health was a receipt.

SOMETHING TOLD ME

Something told me to get my annual physical every top of the year.
Something told me to treat everything I do with integrity.
Something told me that I was born connected.
Something told me to sleep on planes.
Something told me to enjoy the ride.
Something told me that in the end, God will always decide.

PART I

HOPE SCHOLARSHIP

Tell the truth, the truth will set you free and give you victory.

—Pops (in a prison letter)

I

SHOOT HIM IN THE STOMACH AND LET GOD DECIDE

My opportunity to attend an HBCU happened. I was originally planning on going to the University of Memphis, but as you'll read, due to unforeseen circumstances, something happened to change my course.

I was offered a scholarship to Alabama State University (ASU) after high school. I had friends and other folks I knew from home who went there. ASU was an obvious transition for a good number of us because it's only two hours from Atlanta. I moved to Montgomery after a summer of hustling. I'm talking morning til night. Trapping, street life, whatever it took.

The summer before college, me and my homeboy Chi took turns trapping. We hooped and we trapped, that was it. That was the gospel.

Every day we'd hoop at different apartments. This was

when real hoopers moved throughout the city to test their game out. Real hoopers walked into somebody else's neighborhoods and took over the courts. This was one of the ways to make a name for yourself. The more you proved you were willing to lock horns with anybody from anywhere, the more your reputation rang through the city.

We had a twenty-four-hour basketball facility called Run N' Shoot on Metropolitan Parkway. Everybody from Atlanta knows about Run N' Shoot. Even if it was four in the morning, you could leave a craps game or a friend's house and go play basketball because it was open twenty-four hours seven days a week. Lord knows who you might run into depending on what time you pulled up.

Run N' Shoot had about sixteen full courts, a track, a gym, and a place to eat. The AND1 phenomenon Hot Sauce used to damn near spend the night in that motherfucker. Him and a lot of other folks honed their skills there. It was actually a dream concept, and it kept a lot of us out of trouble. Instead of getting into trouble or going to the Waffle House and wilding out, we could pull up and play ball no matter what time it was.

Another way to make a name for yourself was trapping. Walk into somebody else's neighborhood and take over the trap. I happened to be great at hooping and trapping. Me and Chi never hooped together because somebody had to stay in the trap. If he was out on the courts, I'd be back in the trap, and vice versa. I was a much better hooper than Chi, but I understood him wanting to go out and get his shots up. I knew my game had to be right for college, but the streets still had a lot of the things I was looking for: people, power, money. I had been moving packs and already been locked up a few times. I was eighteen. My pops was locked up and me and mom landed in College Park. You should know, College Park can put something different in your blood and teach you different ways on how to move.

When I got to Montgomery, my chest was real big-city like, like since I was from Atlanta, I was from the future. I had been hip on cutting-edge fashion, lingo, and trapping. I was a time traveler waiting to see what Alabama had for me. Coming from the mud, I had always knew how to get it from the mud. If you don't pay attention, you'll miss it. You won't get it.

I'd always known that if I was born in Colorado, I would've been the best snowboarder in the world; that if I was born in Hawaii, I would've been the best surfer in the world; but I was raised in College Park, Georgia, so by the time I got to college, I was the best hustler in the world. I'd learned to adapt and thrive in my environment. I became a master of the art of survival.

I used to think it was the game I learned from the voices around me growing up that made me one of the biggest pieces on the chessboard. Those voices were the folks in my neighborhood. Sometimes they came from a man down the street, or a woman at the corner store. Sometimes they came from one of my homeboys, or a neighborhood old head. Sometimes they came from a gas station attendant who'd be like, "Be safe out here," or "So and so was just in here looking for you." Sometimes they came from my mama's boyfriends who called me Killa or Ty. Since I was young, voices had always spoke to me and wrapped me like a fur coat in the middle of winter.

Voices had always tried to protect me. I soon learned there had always been another voice looking to break through. A voice I didn't know what to do with or how to decipher. There had always been another voice coming from a higher place, a higher plane. Sometimes when that voice came to me, I'd talk back. I can't lie, sometimes my mom probably thought I was tripping, asking herself, "Why is my son in his room talking to himself?" Ha.

College was the start of a new chapter. I was at ASU to hoop. At this particular time, I think my declared major was computers or computer programming. Here I am, a freshman. The coaches were compassionate about me getting arrested for selling weed. The Acadome (Dunn-Oliver) was huge, which I saw on my initial visit. I couldn't wait to hoop in there. I had three cars at the time: a Box Chevy, a Cadillac DeVille, and a Ford Expedition. Despite being on a scholarship, when I first got to Montgomery, I did what I knew, I hustled. I sold ounces of mid for like fifty dollars. It was actually a nice little hustle because people thought they were getting a deal, when actually, I was shorting them on the grams. The packs were only like twenty-five grams but for some reason nobody ever complained. I don't know if it was because I had a different kind of vibe than they were used to or something else. Either way, it was a win-win to me: They got new work, I got paid. Everybody left the situation happy.

My roommate was my guy, Robert. Robert got to ASU a year before me. He was one of the biggest reasons I committed to going there. Me and Robert played ball in high school together. When I talked to him about the opportunity to play at ASU, he vouched for the school and the team. "Yeah man, it's cool down here. We got a nice little team, and niggas from Atlanta get plenty love down here." That spoke to me.

The first couple weeks of the semester, me and Robert shared a little dorm room. It was quaint, not much to it, your typical dorm. It worked for us. We didn't do much besides chill around the student union, eat good food, and hoop. I ran my little money plays, and that was pretty much life at the start of the semester.

Everything was fine until the damn toilets on our floor overran and flooded everything, I mean everything. People were mad as hell, and me and Robert weren't an exception. I mean, folks were duck-walking in sandals, splashing water all throughout the damn dorm floor. It all got real nasty real fast; shit became a mess. Me and Robert had to figure something out. We had only been living there a couple weeks, but it definitely was no place for a player like me or my Ralph Lauren Polo collection. When maintenance came through, they said it would take a couple of weeks to get everything back in order. Man hell nah, that wasn't going to work. We had to do something. I had to put my pack-selling money to work. We had to move off campus, and that's exactly what we did.

We moved and got a smooth little apartment not too far from everything. We were comfortable, and the basketball season hadn't started yet. I was going to classes, dressing fly, wearing fly cologne, and riding fly whips. I drove three different cars every week, hung around the yard, mingled with the ladies, sold some weed, and even gambled. It actually was real fun. I built relationships and watched some grow fast.

It felt like a long way from Atlanta, farther than a couple of hours. Thinking back, it actually was due to its different pace. If I viewed myself as a time traveler from the future, I had started to learn and enjoy my temporary home. Things were simple, not much to choose from, not much going on. There were a few local eateries, hangout spots, and entertainment places. It was nothing like Atlanta, nothing like a big city. But it had slowly started to grow on me. And even though I had only been in Montgomery for a little over a month, it had started to feel like I was exactly where I was supposed to be.

ASU was one of those campuses that the community flocked to. It didn't matter if you were a student or not, hanging out on campus and around the student union was the place for the city. You'd see a lot of the locals hanging out, banging music, or shooting their shot to see if a vulnerable ear might be open to game. That was life. One afternoon, me and Robert were hanging out near the union, and Robert told me some locals wanted to talk to me. He said they had something they thought I might be interested in. Rims.

"Bruh and nem said they got some rims for like five hundred," Robert said, leaning in smiling big because he knew me. He knew I'd for sure be interested. I mean, if you weren't riding heavy in the mid-to-late nineties, then you won't understand how essential rims were. Cars and rims went hand in hand. Imagine wearing a nice outfit with tore-up shoes, or eating a lobster tail off a basic Dixie Ultra plate. In the mid-to-late nineties, it didn't matter what kind of car you drove or even how clean it was, if it wasn't sitting on something, then you wasn't doing shit.

"Hell yeah, I want to see what they're talking about. When can we go see them?" I looked over in the direction Robert had been staring. They definitely were some dudes we had seen before. When I think back on it all, I remember them being some ugly motherfuckers too. One dude in particular. He was just a real ugly-ass nigga. I should've known he was up to no good. If God made a nigga that looked like that, then I should've known something was up. He couldn't have been getting any fucking with his whole life. I should've known he was up to no good.

We exchanged numbers and made plans with the guys to see the rims later that night. While we waited back at our apartment, I remember everything being eerily calm. Too calm. Most days, folks would be stopping by, or we'd be outside dribbling talking shit. But not that night. That night, me and Robert chilled on the couch watching ESPN reruns and didn't say much. It was a hot and humid late-summer day. Might've been a Thursday. Our fans were being pushed to the limits, and we couldn't drink enough water. I remember that hypnotic sound of the fans spinning. I wondered if the rims spun, too. Wondered how large they were and which one of my cars they'd look the meanest on.

Before we left, I paced my bedroom. I don't think I was nervous. Maybe I was. I knew I was ready to get everything over with. I suppose there was some excitement in there somewhere. And then familiar silence settled in. A silence followed by a familiar voice that had been trying to break through. Listen. It's hard to explain something you have absolutely no reference for. Nobody ever talked about voices where I'm from. I would imagine if anybody had, the hood would've called them crazy and said they were on that shit. Probably would've asked them to dance like Gator in Spike Lee's *Jungle Fever*. And while I couldn't explain what I was hearing, I knew it was from deep within. And whatever it was, I knew it felt familiar, it was something like me. Not the voice of the folks in the neighborhood I grew up in. It wasn't the voice of the man down the street or the woman at the corner store. It wasn't the voice of my homeboys, or the neighborhood old head. It wasn't the gas station attendant or one of my mama's boyfriends. This voice was different. This voice was in my head. This voice was trying to tell me something.

The clock had hit the time we agreed on, and we headed to the apartment complex to see the rims. Before leaving, *something told me* to put some money in my sock. *Don't put it in your pockets. Not this time, not tonight.* It also told me to put some money in my crotch. *Put the rest in your pants, that's the new stash spot.* Never take a situation for granted. Always be on point and know that even the kindest nigga can turn on you. Even though I had no idea who the fuck was talking to me, I did what the voice told me to.

The ride was calm. We rode with the windows cracked and a cool little breeze flowed through the Box Chevy. Robert's demeanor was normal. He drove with one hand on the wheel and a Newport in the other. I fired up a blunt and relaxed my shoulders. The closer we got to the complex, the more I started to smile. I had to get it out the way because I couldn't let them know I was too excited. I was about to be shining. Montgomery was about to have a problem on their hands.

When we got to the apartment building, which was in the trenches of Montgomery, we noticed a lot of the streetlights were off or had been knocked out. It was dark, still muggy. Very calm, no dogs barking or nothing, didn't hear none of that.

The guys had told us they'd meet us near the south side of the building. We had precise orders: *Pull up in the parking lot on the north side of the building. Call us once you're parked. Walk up the steps in the front and there will be a walkway. Follow that to the back of the building.* I remember seeing some OGs who nodded in our direction, "You boys good?" The complex was one of those multigenerational ones filled with Black occupants. The ones where grandma lives on the third floor, her daughter lives on the second, and the daughter's ex-husband lives on the first.

"How clean you think these motherfuckers about to be?" I said, looking over at Robert while we moved down the walkway.

"Shit, you about to be shining. I hope these Alabama bumpkins got they shades ready." We laughed. We eased around the side of the complex toward the back. The farther we got from the Box Chevy, the less excited I felt. My spirit was feeling a sense of unease, and I didn't know why. It's strange how a bunch of things can be happening all at once. How we can find ourselves walking, and with every step, be tied to other outcomes than the ones we expected.

That voice in my head from earlier had returned, and with every step we took, the voice got louder. The first thing the voice said to me was: *There are no rims, there are no rims.* That came through as clear as anything I've ever heard in my life. When I heard it, I looked over at Robert, but his mouth wasn't moving. Knowing that it wasn't Robert speaking raised the volume of the voice in my head. We took another step, and the decibel grew louder. We took one more step, then boom.

"You know what the fuck time this is. Come on with the money, mayne," the voice barked out of nowhere.

I almost thought he was joking, like it was some kind of prank just to fuck with us. I was confused because if he was serious, then he had to know we knew who he was. There were several of them from earlier in the day, and as expected, the ugliest of all the ugly niggas was the one doing the talking, the one holding the gun. Me and Robert stood frozen, not really knowing what to say or do.

"Niggas did you hear what I just said? Come on with the motherfucking money," he said again, but this time raising the gun to the sky then smashing it into the right side of Robert's head. Robert immediately hit a knee. And before I could say or do anything, the pistol was in my face.

"What money? Ain't nobody even got nothing," I pleaded, not making any eye contact.

"Naw fuck that. Y'all niggas come off all that money."

"We just wanted to see the rims. We didn't even come here to get 'em." I felt the scratch of money against my ankles. The rustle of money against my balls.

"Don't fucking play with me. You niggas trying to get shot? Get yo ass on the ground." He patted my pockets but didn't find anything.

I laid on my stomach and wondered if this might be it for me. I thought of my mama, who was my best friend, and all my people back home, everyone who celebrated me off to college. I thought of my pops and how he signed every letter with "God is love." I laid on my stomach wondering where God was. Was He in Atlanta tending to some other business while I laid on my stomach about to lose my life?

I shut my eyes and imagined the headline: STUDENT ATHLETE TAUHEED EPPS FOUND ON THE SOUTH SIDE OF

AN APARTMENT COMPLEX IN THE MIDDLE OF BUTTFUCK, MONTGOMERY, ALABAMA. HE WAS FOUND WITH A BAND IN HIS SOCKS AND A STASH IN HIS NUTTS.

On October 23, 1989, a white Bostonian named Charles Stuart called 911 and reported that he and his wife had been shot. He told dispatch that the couple were heading home from a childbirth class when a Black man entered their car, demanded their property, and ultimately shot his pregnant wife, Carol, in the head and him in the stomach before fleeing. Now, Charles was in such distress that he couldn't make out exactly where the couple was and eventually passed out as the dispatcher was working to get more information about their location. When the couple was finally found, it was near the Mission Hill neighborhood of Boston.

Carol Stuart would die at Brigham and Women's Hospital later that night, but the baby would survive for over two weeks. Charles Stuart would survive the attack and identify the assailant as a Black man in a tracksuit with stripes. This sparked a ton of racial tension. You have to think about it. In the mid-1970s, Boston experienced a ton of racial aggression over antibusing protests. This led to a number of Black schoolchildren attending predominantly white schools being assaulted. In the eighties, when it came to racial matters, Boston was at best a delicate city. You can imagine the tension when its residents learned that a Black man murdered a pregnant white woman and shot her unarmed husband right around the corner from the projects. There was no way this would end in justice without retribution.

In attempting to hunt down the assailant, the police stormed the Mission Hill projects and terrorized their community in search of the Black man wearing the tracksuit with stripes. The problem was, this was during the time when Run-D.M.C. and other rappers had made Adidas striped tracksuits fashionable. If the police were looking for a Black man wearing that outfit, they could throw a rock and hit one. There were reports of police busting down the doors of Black families and leaving homes in shambles. Many filed complaints, talking about the ways their civil rights had been violated and the ways their sons had been profiled.

For the people in the Mission Hill community, the story never seemed right. They said it out loud to themselves. *Let me get this shit straight: A Black man in a tracksuit robbed a white couple and shot a pregnant woman in the head around the corner from the projects he fled to? And not only that, but the husband, who was much larger in stature than the wife, did not receive a fatal shot and lived to talk about it?* This didn't sound right at all to the Mission Hill community. As the investigation continued, several suspects had been interviewed and one publicly prosecuted. It wasn't until Charles Stuart's brother, Matthew, confessed to the police that Charles had actually shot both Carol and himself and staged it to look like a robbery. Matthew admitted how he assisted Charles in this plan by disposing of Carol's belongings and the gun that Charles used to shoot his wife in the head and himself in the stomach. The morning after Matthew confessed, that coward Charles Stuart jumped off the Tobin Bridge.

"I'm telling you, we don't have shit," I repeated over and over. Everything was happening so fast, and at some point, they must've believed us because they ran off into the dark. Then it got quiet again. Me and Robert both on our stomachs, both breathing heavy.

"Robert you good, you straight?"

"Yeah Ty, I'm good."

"Man, let's get the fuck up out of here."

These guys tried to rob us and we knew exactly who they were. That bothered me most. It was an attempted robbery because they didn't get anything from either of us.

None of that mattered. I was hot. I wanted revenge. I wanted smoke. I'm from Atlanta, and I felt like those country-ass niggas done tried me. I wanted to make an example out of them before word got around that I was sweet. I couldn't go out like that. The disrespect. I needed revenge bad. I didn't want a fistfight; I didn't want to square up. He drew his pistol on me, I wanted to draw a pistol on him. That's how I felt. I wanted my lick back. As we left, we had the windows cracked. The ride back to our apartment was just as quiet as the ride to the attempted robbery. Robert was smoking a cigarette, I wasn't smoking nothing. I was just thinking, *This nigga done tried us.*

I had drama thoughts in my head until we got back to our apartment. But my first phone call wasn't to my folks back home to discuss revenge. It wasn't to tell my niggas to armor up and get their asses over to Montgomery. It wasn't to put the trap on alert that it was time to go to war. Nope, that wasn't my first call. My first call went out to my best friend. My first call went to my mama.

"Mama, these niggas done tried to rob me." My voice shook as I was saying it.

"Lord have mercy. You alright? Robert alright?"

"Yeah we good, we good. We good. Just shook up, you know?"

"I'm sorry that happened to you, Ty. Don't go and do nothing crazy, okay? Why don't you come home and get away from Montgomery for a while."

The next day I drove to Atlanta with the intentions of gathering a crew to take back with me to handle the situation. While I was hashing out retaliation in my mama's kitchen, my pops called from prison because he'd heard about everything.

"Aye Pop, these guys tried to rob me and Robert."

"What you mean they tried to rob y'all?"

"Yeah. We had went over to look at some rims, and they upped a pistol on us, hit Robert in the head and everything. Made us both get down."

"What you doing getting robbed at college? You supposed to be there in school."

"I know. And the most fucked-up part is that we know who did it."

"What you mean y'all know who did it?"

"Yeah. We know who did it. Some ugly-ass local niggas."

"Son, listen to me carefully. You need to go get you a gun."

"That's what I was thinking, but I can also have some people handle this for me."

"No. Go get *you* a gun. Handle it yourself. Walmart got guns. Walmart got shotguns, and you don't have to wait, you can buy them on the spot." There was a pause and for a moment neither of us said anything.

"I'm listening, Pop."

"After you get your gun, you don't have to try and kill him, but he could die. It won't be your decision either way. Get you a gun and some bullets, then go find him. When you see who did it, don't think, just shoot. Shoot him in the stomach and let God decide."

II

WOMEN ARE BORN SUPERHEROES

I was raised primarily by my mom. My pops had been in and out of prison since I can remember. Pops used to tell me a woman couldn't raise a man. Sometimes during our phone calls while he was locked up, he'd say things like, "Son, keep your head on a swivel and take care of yourself. I mean, you know I'm here for you, but I can't be there right now. I'm always willing to talk about anything anytime. But just remember that a woman can't raise a man."

After those conversations I'd tell my mom what he said. She really didn't pay much attention to it and would tell me not to listen. "Don't listen to him," she'd say. "I think I'm doing a really good job."

And she was. She was doing a hell of a job. This was usually a moment for me and her to bond, to connect. For us to be reminded of our incredible closeness, to be reminded of how for most of my life, it had been us two against everything.

I believed my pops's sentiments came from an old-school way of thinking. We knew this and didn't judge him. It had to be difficult watching me move in a dangerous environment, knowing his full support had metal bars blocking it. While phone calls provided a certain level of guidance, his physical presence would've provided more. Pops watched from behind metal bars.

He watched me morphing into something special and wasn't able to take credit for what I was becoming. I knew he wanted to have a bigger hand in everything. I knew how much he loved me, how much I loved him. He was my dog.

No matter what my pops said about my mom raising me, we never held it against him. We were always too busy moving forward. We knew if we weren't moving forward, nobody was coming to save us. There weren't any superheroes in capes flying in to save us. Our outcome relied on what we could do for ourselves, me and mom.

I believe every woman in the world is born with some type of intuition. You know, they're just born with it. I actually think everyone is born with it, but women tap into the power of their intuition a lot earlier than men. Women mature quicker than men, too.

My mom has always been a very strong woman. Charismatic, but also has a little bully edge to her, meaning she don't play that shit. She's always known how things would turn out before they happened. The time I did get locked up in high school, she told me not to take all those drugs to school. (More on this in the next chapter.) The time I almost got robbed in Montgomery, she told me not to take all them cars to school. Countless times, she laid out a map for which direction to go, a game plan.

Her mother was a real gangster. My grandmother sold

bootleg liquor, shot at police, and was a real badass. My mother has actually told me that I'm the one who broke the generational chains. Her grandmother sold bootleg stuff, her grandfather sold bootleg stuff, her mama sold bootleg stuff, my mama sold illegal stuff. My mama fell in love with a dope dealer, they got married and sold dope together. Eventually they had me. An only child. A former dope dealer.

More than being a gangster, my grandmother was a very strong Black woman. She was the first superhero I came to know. I remember seeing her all the time in these big, long, flowing gowns. Those were her capes. When she was wearing one of those, food was normally on the way.

She made the best pancakes I have ever had, to this day—that's actually a superpower in itself. Them damn pancakes. There had to be some kind of superhero super-sauce in them things, you hear me? Them things would be fluffy, soft, but have the crispy edges, completely melt in your mouth. Everybody was on their best behavior on mornings we smelled pancakes in the air, even my grandfather.

My mother's father, my grandfather, was named EF. He was a tall man who stood about six-three. He never really said much. He was a quiet man who loved baseball. Especially the Braves. He actually played in the Negro League. What I remember most about EF was that he was always in his work clothes, Carhartt jackets and overalls. He had that old school work ethic. I remember my cousin used to point at the E and the F on the gas gauges whenever we got in a car and say, "that's our grandaddy name."

My grandparents lived next to a church. You could

actually hear the sermons on Sundays during football even if you didn't go. Could hear people saying, "Well, well, thank you Lord, amen." Could hear the choir covering the neighborhood like the blood of Christ. Reverend Tucker was the preacher. Everybody loved them some Reverend Tucker. He was the messenger.

My grandmother would go to church sometimes and sometimes she would stay home. I remember being intimidated by her because she was a bit more heavyset. She had a physical presence about her, and I had also heard stories about how she used to put her hands on people, including my mom. I remember thinking, *If my mom is somebody you don't fuck with, and my grandmother beat her up, what does that make my grandmother?* I also knew for a fact that she had to have some kind of superpower to still be alive, as wild as she lived. Her name was Ernestine.

My pops's mom was another one of the first superheroes I came to know. Her name was Grace. She worked for Avon, the global skincare and cosmetics company. Avon promoted pink as one of its brand colors. I know at some point it started to be called "power pink," but I'm unsure if it was called that when my grandmother worked for them. Everything around her was pink: her clothes, her shoes, her accessories.

She would make these incredible fish sticks. That was one of her superpowers. They didn't taste like frozen, store-bought fish sticks, though I'm guessing they had to be. Hers were gourmet. Imagine if Ruth's Chris had a fish-stick option. She would put them in the oven, but she had to do something else with them because them motherfuckers were delicious. Anytime I went over there, I'd damn near pray that my grandmother would make some fish sticks. I didn't even need a side or nothing, the fish sticks were enough.

Now my granddaddy, my father's dad, wanted me to be smart. He would push me to think critically and quiz me on things. He wanted me to read encyclopedias, talk about the almanac, help him paint the porch, help him in the garden. He'd work me to death in the heat and talk about my pops like he was a dog.

"You know your father is probably going back to jail again soon. I wish he would get his life together. Take care of his responsibilities like a grown man."

I never said anything back, I just listened. That was his testimony, and there was nothing he could say to cause me to see my pops as anything other than a role model.

My grandmother Grace rarely talked. She was such a nice woman but quiet. She even laughed silently. I would see tears in her eyes, but her laugh wouldn't make a sound. Sometimes I didn't even know what she'd be laughing at. I remember asking her so many times, "Grandma, what you laughing at?" and she'd just be sitting there, laughing under her breath.

I used to have to open her car door because she had arthritis in her thumbs. She had a Chevy Nova or something, a clean car. I used to ride with her a lot. Sometimes we'd ride in silence, but I could still feel a constant hug coming from the driver's seat. She had the ability to hug you without touching you. That was a superpower.

She was the sweetest thing in the world, but a hardworking professional. I wonder if that's where I get my business savvy from. I heard many stories about how she was the first Black woman with Avon to do all these incredible things and break all these sales records. She was very headstrong, but also very, very humble. I wonder if that's where I get my humility from.

My mom was the second superhero I came to know but the first I could actually touch. She literally turned nothing into something so many times. More than a superhero, maybe she's more like a magician. She always figured out ways to figure it out.

No matter what was going on, she made sure I stayed strong, that I stayed hopeful. Those times when there wasn't anything to eat, she would convince me that hunger was all in my head. That no matter what was going on, I would be fine as long as I stayed focused on hope and we had each other. That still sticks with me until this day when it comes to my wife and kids; no matter what in the world is going on, we gone stay hopeful, and we gone stay together.

My pops was my role model, which made him a superhero too. I loved my pops. His superpowers were different. He was a tough, hardcore-street-reputation-type dude. Everybody in the hood knew not to fuck with my pops. This made him a superhero to me. My mom was tough too. But she also had the power of intuition. She could see the future. She would say shit like, "Ty, watch the company you keep" and "Always be yourself," if she ever felt I was moving in a way that didn't truly represent the person she raised. It was always something I was aware of but not completely.

I made the connections between her premonitions and the things that happened, but I never put it all together. I never sat back and thought, *Damn, my mom is intuitive.* I didn't even use that word growing up.

When I was a senior in high school, she walked into my

room and caught me bagging up weed for school and told me she didn't think it was a good idea. Her concern didn't have to do with me selling weed. She'd known for years I was trapping. She was one of the first people to put work in my hands. That wasn't the issue. The issue was the amount I'd planned to take with me. Something about going to school with that much weed on me didn't feel right to her. *Something told her* the next day would be horrible for me. She was right (more about this in the next chapter).

Women are born superheroes with a unique ability to connect with their intuition. In my life, women have always been more in tune with their intuition than the men I know. My wife Kesha used to own a day care and could tell me the kids who were about to catch a cold every cold season. Not only did she know the kids who would catch a cold, but she also knew the strain. She was never wrong. She also knew when something wasn't going right in a kid's home based on the kid's behavior. She could tell if kids were around negative or positive influences. Whenever I asked how she knew, she would casually say, "I had a feeling."

We were celebrating a family member's birthday one afternoon, and Kesha's cousin, a first cousin who was like a sister to her, was really late arriving. It was odd to us because everybody expected her there on time. There were some events that had occurred earlier that day that signaled to my wife that something wasn't right.

We were at my mom's house. It was a pool party. I remember it clearly. Everybody was having fun, but my wife was caught up in a different emotional space. Something didn't feel right. *Something told her* to go check on her cousin. She went. When Kesha got to her cousin's house, she knocked a couple of times, but then quickly got out of there. She would later explain to me that she felt something, like an energy, an energy that scared the shit out of her. She came back to my mom's house until *something told her* to go back. I went with her this time. And when we got there, we found that her cousin had been murdered. Apparently there had been a domestic situation and she was killed by her estranged boyfriend. That man had also kidnapped her three daughters and done unspeakable things to them. That was a hard time for our family.

Sometimes you'll hear women say, "*Something was telling me* to leave that no-good nigga alone. I knew from the start he wasn't good for me, but I kept on seeing him. Why didn't I listen?" They might say this after calling it quits with some guy. *Something told them* not to get involved from the start. The same can be said when men get with a woman and from the start have a gut feeling that she might not be good for you. You might still get involved with her knowing that the outcome might be sketchy. Nine times out of ten it is because you didn't listen to your inner voice.

When we hear people say "*something told me,*" we tend to brush it off as coincidence or hindsight. I have never believed in coincidences, but I believe that the "something" we feel, or sometimes hear, is coming from a higher place; that something is coming from God. It took years for me to arrive here, but my life story has been my testimony. When I look back on my life and the times I've been saved from terrible outcomes, it was because I listened to the intuitive voice inside me, the *something*. Remember when *something told me* to put my money in my sock before going to see those rims? Had I not listened, that money was gone.

Michelle Obama said this about how she was able to have the incredible career she's had: "When I was in college, I thought I wanted to be a lawyer because it sounded like a job for good, respectable people. It took me a few years to listen to my intuition and find a path that fit better for who I was, inside and out." Intuition is a powerful voice that guides us. We just need to listen to it.

The great Harriet Tubman said she experienced visions and dreams that guided her during her efforts to free Black people. None of this is to say that any of us will become Michelle Obama or Harriet Tubman. I'm only emphasizing the importance of listening to the higher voice we might hear or feel but don't know how to name. We're not crazy. You're not crazy.

Remember in the creation story when God tells Adam that he and Eve shouldn't eat from the tree of knowledge? He wasn't indirect at all. God's voice and instructions to Adam were clear: "But of the tree of the knowledge of good and evil you shall not eat, for in the day that you eat of it you shall surely die." What if that voice has never gone away? What if we just moved further from our ability to hear it? What if we're all born with a divine compass that breaks through when we don't know where the hell we are or where the hell we're going? That's been a truth for many who are tuned and tapped into it (think radio frequency).

It requires practice. It comes easier for some than for others. Without that voice or that intuitive something, Harriet Tubman might not have led captives out of unspeakable bondage.

III

STARSHIP ON OLD NATIONAL

My senior year of high school I was mostly about basketball and money. If you saw me, you probably saw a basketball close by. And if you really saw me, there was probably some money around. I can't say I was any different from a lot of the people I knew. We all had ideas about how to move our family situations forward. When you're raised in the trap, you can find yourself dodging traps, contemplating how to move beyond the circumstances consuming you.

It wasn't like I didn't love my neighborhood and the people in it. I loved my people. Trunks rattling on a hot-ass summer day. Weed smoke circling in the air. The trap had love in it every single day. That love isn't talked about nearly enough.

That stated, I didn't love the limitations, the violence, the pain, the hopelessness. It was always in me to make sure me and my mama had a way out. I wanted us to see the world. I wanted us to see the world and then come back to the trap and report on everything we saw. I had started selling weed in middle school. High school was no different. Being a star on the basketball team didn't put bread on the table. That was a fact. And being a star on the basketball team didn't stop me from hanging out in stores that felt like spaceships.

This story begins on a late Thursday afternoon and my going to Starship Enterprises to grab weed baggies. If you were never inside a Starship Enterprises store in the mid-nineties, you definitely missed out on something. Starship was a chain, a novelty chain (I'm pretty sure they're still around). They had everything from porn to paraphernalia, to T-shirts, bongs, scales, chains, whips, whatever you can name, any and everything to keep a young man's attention—it was extravagant. Think *ATLiens* and *Aquemini* Outkast. That's what it felt like in there. Like you walked into an Outkast album.

We would go in there to check out their latest stuff. I remember they had these little stash cans and stash spots for drugs. We'd go in, look at their new inventory, and eventually spend money. The layout was like any other department store, but the décor was definitely different. The isles were lit up neon-rainbow, and their logo was a big-ass spaceship, outlined in purple and pink. The marketing strategy had to be, "If you're looking for smoke, kink, or choke, we got you." They sold every kind of debauchery item you could imagine: lingerie, costumes, bondage restraints, lubricants, sex toys.

To keep it a hundred, I was just trying to make some

money. By my senior year, I was going to school on my own. My mom was no longer waking me up in the mornings. Well, technically she never woke me up. She would just come into my room in the morning and turn the light on. That would normally be enough to wake me up. By the time I got to high school, she stopped doing that. I got up on my own. I was self-motivated in the mornings. I actually enjoyed school, I enjoyed learning, I enjoyed being around people. I've always been an extrovert, always preferred socializing. I also preferred looking fresh and having my outfits together. That required money. My senior year I had been doing well in school. I made As and Bs and was gearing up to take the SAT.

I hadn't been in a hurry to take the SAT because I felt like I had good test-taking skills. It was a requirement for me to secure a basketball scholarship, but I never believed I'd need to take it more than once. I figured I'd take the test and be good after that. I didn't need to rehearse. That Thursday afternoon I got a little weed in.

I went to Starship because I'd heard about some brand-new weed baggies. I remember walking in with my homeboy and the employees being like "what up?" because they'd known me. They knew what I was about and what I was on. They knew I was a trapper. I was a regular. I'd like to explain my movement that day in military terms. When we walked into Starship, the register was at eleven o'clock. To my right, about two o'clock, there was all the porn party supplies. And then to my left, about nine o'clock, were the new baggies. When we came in, I made a left, right to the new baggies. My homeboy made a right, right toward the new porn. That nigga was a freak.

The new baggies were more vertical than horizontal.

Think of today's weed packaging and how folks can now sell product more according to how the packaging looks. That's how the new baggies were. They had a new kind of look. I've always been into marketing since a very early age, so I knew the baggies would sell themselves off the look. We called the horizontal baggies pillow sacks. Everybody had been using pillow sacks for a while. These were longer, sleeker, and most importantly, new.

If I knew anything about anybody, I knew niggas loved new shit: shoes, records, cars, girls, etc. And I was willing to bet they'd love new bags. It didn't matter that the weed would be the same, the new bags were enough to convince them they were smoking something new. Marketing has always been one of my strengths. The new baggies were a way for me to rebrand.

We left Starship right around the time the sun left the sky. It was getting dark, and I needed to get everything bagged up. My pops was in prison my senior year. Right before he got locked up, he'd won a green Mercury Grand Marquis. It was old school. He'd won a raffle or something in LaGrange, Georgia. The raffle came with a car. He called me right before going in and said, "Son, go get the car." I went and got it earlier that year, and it had been mine since. It was heavy and long. On the outside it looked like a true pimp mobile, like a true player had to be the owner. But it had its hang-ups: the carpet floors and vinyl-covered upholstery. The ashtray had seen too many bodies so there was that smell underneath the air fresheners.

But that wasn't the worst. The worst was that it didn't have power steering. That was the worst. I damn near feel like right now my biceps and triceps came from driving that fucking car. We left Starship in that car. I dropped my homeboy off and muscled the wheels back to the house. When I walked in, my mom was knocking out dishes.

"Big Saturday coming up? Right Ty?" My mom has always called me Ty, short for Tauheed. She was talking about the SAT, but I wasn't thinking about the test at all. I was locked in on the weed I needed to bag before bed. The house was quiet, which was on par for a Thursday night. I was supposed to take the SAT Saturday morning. It was just a formality. I'd been the consummate honor roll student; learning came easy for me. The SAT was just another thing to do. I had never been a dummy in school. I flossed As like new shoes. I got my first C in college, and literally had to try. I wanted to see what being average felt like. It sounds crazy, but it was a game I wanted to play. I wasn't trying to mock the system or nothing like that. I just needed to know what getting a C felt like. I got a C by simply not going to class.

I went to my room to start bagging the weed but was devastated when my Digi Scale malfunctioned. It completely stopped calibrating. Out of nowhere. I'd put a nickel on it, and instead of reading point-five grams, the screen wouldn't read shit. My world was ending. My mind was racing because I knew I didn't have a lot of time. If you've never sold drugs, you wouldn't know how it feels to get new work. And if you've never gotten new work, you wouldn't know the high of finding a new way to market it. I had new work, I had new baggies, but I didn't have a functioning fucking Digi Scale, and that truth was a tragedy.

When you're a trap nigga, you can pay to borrow somebody's scale. You can't just go around using people's scales, that's not how it works. You have to give up something. I walked around our apartment complex looking to find a scale to borrow. For some reason, I kept coming up short. It was like everybody was out in the streets that night, and the people around didn't have shit.

All the stores were closed, and for some reason *something told me* to get in touch with Big Bo. To this day I don't know how I found him, but I did. Big Bo had a triple beam scale. I had never used one. My pops had a triple beam. I like to bring the scale up because I feel like that scale jinxed me. And I haven't used a triple beam since.

It was like I lucked up but was fucked up because he stayed a little far from me. This meant I had to get back in the Grand Marquis and drive a minute. I didn't care. Nothing was going to stop me from bagging that night. I can't say it wasn't a chore though. I had been used to battery-operated digital scales. Triple beams are like those doctor's scales that make you measure until the weight is right. It's much more time-consuming, but I didn't have a choice. Thinking back on it, I have no idea why I didn't try putting a battery in my digital scale. It probably was an easy fix. I guess it doesn't matter now. Things go the way they're supposed to.

Nobody can convince me that Bo's triple beam scale wasn't a jinx. The moment I got that scale to my bedroom, *something told me* not to use it. It wasn't because I didn't know how it worked, or that I was worried about weighing the weed wrong. Something about the damn scale seemed like it had been cursed. Like it had ghosts around it. Bo's old-ass scale should've had its funeral. It had weighed enough dope. I didn't know about its past. Maybe it had gotten Bo rich or somebody he'd known rich. Or maybe it had done just enough work to get niggas through some hard times.

Either way, its best days were behind it, and my intuition was telling me to just wait. Something was telling me to fix my Digi Scale and get the work off next week. But I was committed, and I didn't listen. Friday had to be the day. Come hell or high water, I was getting that shit off.

My mom must've felt something was off too. I had almost finished bagging everything when she opened my door and saw everything I had going on. She saw all the weed in all those new baggies. It was actually only about a hundred dollars' worth, but all the nick sacks made it look like a lot. My mom stood in the doorway watching me concentrate on the last few baggies. She saw me putting that old-ass gigantic scale to work.

"Boy, what is you doing? Where you about to take all this weed?"

"To school tomorrow."

"That's a lot of damn weed, Ty. Why are you taking so much?"

"Tomorrow Friday, Mom. These folks gone buy this weed."

"I understand that, but why are you taking so much? That's a lot of weed, Ty."

"Everybody wants weed on Fridays for the weekend. I usually sell out. Bet I won't sell out tomorrow. I got enough work for everybody."

She left my room but not before giving me one last look that let me know I was fucking up.

The thing about our relationship was that she trusted me to know what I was doing. She trusted my instincts and leadership capabilities. We had been through so much and our survival had never meant playing it safe. Our lives had been like any game of chance, sometimes we won and sometimes we didn't. My mom knew me better than anybody else in the world, and I could tell by how she looked at me that she knew we'd lose this one. But she never told me no. She never mentioned losing.

My mom's intuition was trying to tell me it wasn't a good idea. She probably didn't know how to articulate it, and I know back then I couldn't imagine how strong her intuition was. I assumed she was just tripping, overreacting. I finished bagging the weed and went to sleep.

The next morning I woke up at the same time I always did and conducted my same morning routine. I wanted to look extra sharp, extra clean. I remember exactly what I wore to school that morning: red Polo chino jacket, cream Polo chino pants, plaid button-down Polo shirt, tucked in, Polo boots—giving drip to North Clayton High School, fashion all the way.

I pulled the green Mercury Grand Marquis into the school's parking lot. I was in a great mood even though the weather was dreary, and my snatch-out car CD player was acting up. I wanted to start getting off my packs before the bell rang and school started.

People knew me, knew my car, and knew that on most Fridays I had work. That was my play, to serve before school, at lunch, and after school. The students would give me their little five dollars, and I'd give them a nick sack. It was easy. Well, it was mostly easy. North Clayton High School had eyes in the sky. By this time, there had been a murder in the parking lot and a suicide inside the school. They were armed with cameras very early on. In fact, North Clayton might've been the first school in Atlanta to have surveillance cameras. We didn't have metal detectors back then, but we fucking did have surveillance.

While this fact made me cautious about how I made my plays that morning, it most certainly didn't stop me. I did what I had to do until the bell rang, and once it did, school started off normal: English first period, math second period, history third period. Nothing was off about the first couple of classes, but at some point during history, something just didn't feel right. I can't explain what it was, but *something told me* the routine nature of that day would soon be changing. And it did.

About halfway through the period, there was a disturbance outside the door. I initially didn't pay it too much attention because I was staring out the window trying to calculate the work I had left. Our history teacher went to the door and started talking to two white guys outside the classroom. The white guys weren't nothing to write home about. I figured they might've been some counselors or maybe we were having some sort of impromptu procedure discussion. I wasn't at all paying them much attention until they started pointing in my direction, motioning me to come to the door. And I did. But once I got close, I realized they were carrying badges. These two motherfuckers were cops. There was nothing I could do. The two white guys smiled at me and said, "Don't run."

We walked to the office to discuss something I knew nothing about. The casual mood during the walk shifted once we got to the principal's office.

"We have reason to believe you're selling something," the older white guy said with this serious-ass face like that shit was supposed to intimidate me or something.

"I don't know what y'all talking about."

"You know we got cameras in this school," the younger one said, trying to look tougher than his uncle.

Of course I knew the school had cameras and of course I moved accordingly all morning. I couldn't imagine them catching me on nothing. My mind did that thing minds do when backtracking everything, every move, every step, in real time. My morning replayed in my head like a drive-in movie. I sat in a mental drop-top and watched me from the time I pulled into the parking lot to the time those white guys walked into our classroom. Everything on the reel seemed clean, almost too perfect.

Until I watched myself follow the white guys out of the class and saw my red Polo jacket still resting on the back of my chair. I looked at the notebook laying on my desk, nothing in there to see, but the jacket had a whole lot to see. In that moment, it seemed like me and the classroom's camera both had a revelation. I had weed and a beeper on the inside of that jacket. We both knew I had fucked up. We both knew my mom had been right.

"I don't know what y'all are talking about," I told the younger guy who didn't look any older than the students at Clayton. I didn't know if he was the police, a student, or both (on some *21 Jump Street* shit). He for sure thought he was Johnny Depp about to make himself a bust to get his little career going.

"Okay Mr. Epps, we'll find it."

They started checking things, starting with my locker. I followed them while they asked me questions. "What time did you get to school?" "What students have you talked to today?" "Were you wearing anything other than the clothes on your body?" Just grilling me.

When they didn't find anything in my locker, we

moved outside to my car. I unlocked the doors, opened the trunk, and watched them rummage through my shit. The way they meticulously went through everything, you would've thought I was Nino Brown from *New Jack City*. Would've thought I had niggas guarding the school, strung-out sophomores smoking crack on the roof, and a penthouse suite somewhere in that motherfucker. Would've thought I was a kingpin.

"Where's the dope, man? Come on and just give it up." The older guy had gotten tired of it all and looked like he was ready for lunch.

"I don't know anything about dope. I'm just a student here, man."

We went back to the principal's office, and they started reviewing the school's camera footage right in front of me. They started from the moment I had first walked in and followed me up until they knocked on the history teacher's door. It was all inevitable. So was my intention to deny, deny, deny.

There was no mistaking the brightness of that red Polo jacket. I had watched myself walk through the school doors, to my locker, and to first period. Watching myself on-screen was weird as fuck. I had already played everything back but now watching it was even more awkward. This was the sequel, and I wanted no parts. I was in two places at the same time. I definitely was there in the principal's office watching the playback, and I was definitely walking around school with that damn red alarm that a blind man would notice. By the time we'd gotten to the end of the footage, we all stared at the jacket and paused for a second. Then, Johnny Depp broke the silence:

"Where is that red jacket, man?"

"That's my older cousin's jacket," I said calmly. And it wasn't a fake calm, I was actually calm. By that point in my life, I had been through much more hostile situations. "I brought it up here to impress this girl."

They didn't believe me for a second and put out an APB for the jacket. I hoped for a different outcome, a Hail Mary, anything to get me out of the situation. A divine intervention where the jacket disappears out the classroom window. But that wasn't happening, and I knew it. My life had been too real for magic. I'd done too much dirt for genies. They were going to get that jacket.

The two white guys went back to the classroom but by that time lunch had started, so the room was locked. I knew that they knew that I knew that they knew my jacket was in that classroom. They were committed and had no problem waiting until the final lunch period was over. When they eventually came back to the principal's office, I knew what time it was. Johnny Depp was carrying the jacket and wearing a smile. I reached into my acting bag and pretended to be shocked: "What! What that got to do with me?"

Depp pulled the weed out of the pocket, and I went into a complete dramatic monologue: "Boy, that shit ain't none of mine. Y'all done planted that. Hell naw. Call my mama. I swear to God, y'all better call my mama." He pulled the beeper out, and I had to claim that. My beeper was my way of making money. I had to get that back no matter what. "Now that's mine. That beeper is mine, but that weed is not mine."

The police went to doing all this dramatic shit, and that's when the real production started. They put me in handcuffs and called my mom. Me and mom lived in an apartment right behind the school, so it didn't take long for her to get there. And boy, once she got there, she became the lead actor and went into an Oscar-worthy performance. Mom went full Mrs. Baker from *Boyz n the Hood*. Remember how she fell out after Ricky got shot? Yeah, that's who my mom channeled. It was so dramatic that I started checking to see if I had been shot. She did a whole scene: "No. No. Not my Ty. Not my baby," she screamed, then started falling out and everything.

The police called one of my closest homeboys to the office to see if he had known anything. My main man Goat, whose real name was Corey, had always held me down no matter what. We'd been tight since the ninth grade, so I wasn't worried about them questioning him. Goat came into the office and before they asked him anything, I showed him my handcuffs. "Man, they in here talking about I'm selling weed." Goat looked at my handcuffs, looked at the cops, looked at the door, and left the school altogether. I looked out the office window and saw my boy sprinting with the Donovan Bailey form. That nigga probably still running.

Because I went to jail that afternoon, I missed my last opportunity to take the SAT the following morning. The irony was that I could've taken the test my junior year. I also had opportunities to take practice tests since I was a student athlete, but I had declined. I didn't believe I needed the practice. I had never even gotten a C in school and believed all I needed was one time to take the test. I knew I'd get the score I needed for a full-ride basketball scholarship. I had already passed the ACT, but I needed the SAT for a basketball scholarship. That opportunity was gone. I got locked up and couldn't take the test. My world had ended.

This was before social media: no Facebook, no Twitter, no Instagram. The coaches recruiting me had no way of knowing what happened. I was overcome with guilt because I knew I would have to lie. I wouldn't tell the coaches what happened. I knew my high school coach might, but I wouldn't. It was extremely overwhelming.

I sat locked up for about a week and a half. That may not sound like a long time, but when you're looking to get a scholarship and it's toward the end of the season, that's a very long time. Coaches look to lock down recruits before losing them to other schools. Every day, hour, minute, second, matters during recruitment season.

My high school coach, James Gwyn, had been covering for me the whole time I was locked up. He had been someone I trusted and always looked out for me. Gwyn persuaded some coaches to come and watch me work out after I'd gotten released. Coaches flew to Atlanta to watch me play individually and run through drills. I remember them asking me to take off my shirt to see how much weight training I'd need in college. They also asked questions about the SAT.

"What happened with your SAT?"

"Your grades look good."

Memphis and other Division I schools watched me work out and interviewed me.

"You looking good man. We're going to put you on a weight program." In a 2012 ESPN article written by Dan Friedell, former Memphis assistant basketball coach Tom Schuberth was quoted as saying: "We had just lost Penny Hardaway and I remember Tauheed was kind of a combination player: a real versatile 2–3 who could maybe play a little point. . . . The only thing that scared us was he was so thin. . . . It wasn't like we'd go look at any old guy, so he had to be pretty talented for us to go over to Atlanta to look at him."

All the questions about me being skinny and them wanting to see me without a shirt on threw me off. I didn't know how to put it into words then, but it was that slavery-auction-block feeling. The questions about the SAT threw me off too. I didn't know how to respond to those. Whenever SAT questions came up, I pretended not to hear. I didn't know what to tell them. But when they asked those questions, I heard my mom's voice from the night she walked into my bedroom and saw me bagging up all that weed: *Boy, what is you doing? Where you about to take all this weed? That's a lot of damn weed, Ty. Why are you taking so much?*

Something had told her, an intuitive voice, that the next day would be fucked-up.

I had regretted not listening to my mom. I regretted that I didn't go to school without weed that Friday and then woke up on Saturday and passed the SAT. I regretted not staying on Memphis's radar and possibly running that show right after Penny had left. I regretted the schools I missed out on, that may have called my coach's office on the first Monday I sat in a jail cell. I regretted my trip to Starship the Thursday before everything went down and Bo's jinxing-ass triple beam scale.

I regretted everything until the day Alabama State's basketball coach, John L. Williams, called out of the blue and said: "Listen, we heard what happened. Don't worry. We'd love to have you down here. We got a full ride for you. Come visit next week and check us out."

And that right there was all I needed to hear. That's

how I ended up in a place that would open up my social butterfly personality and my musical interests. That's where I would meet my wife, who would eventually become the mother of my three beautiful children. The cliché "everything happens for a reason" is real if you believe. It took everything happening for me to end up in Montgomery, Alabama. And now, looking back, I don't regret any of it. I'd take all that weed to school all over again. I'd take being locked up for a week and a half to end up right here.

IV

IT'S A BLESSING TO HAVE A PLUG

After finishing college with a degree in psychology, I went back to hustling in Atlanta. My degree fit me perfectly because I'd always been interested in how people think. It's crazy that two people can look at the same picture but draw very different conclusions. Or, two people can come from the same environment but have very different outcomes depending on a lot of factors, and sometimes how they think can be one of those factors.

We hear the stories all the time. Two people come from the same block; one ends up in prison, the other becomes a world-renowned surgeon. The nature-versus-nurture debate was one of the fascinating concepts we talked about in school. The question of what actually determines who we are. Is it the things already inside us when we're born that are genetic, or is it our environment and the people we meet? Theorists been arguing about this for years, and nobody can prove it one way or another. The one thing I did know after college when I came back to Atlanta was that it was definitely in my nature to be outside in the streets nurturing my income.

I was hustling in the streets of Atlanta. I had already been selling weed and making a little money when I was introduced to my first plug. Thinking back, I've had two and a half plugs in my life. One of them we didn't do business long together, so that plug is not worth mentioning. A plug is the person you get your product from. That could be weed, crack, coke, pills. It was weed for me. I needed somebody to supply me weed in bulk. If you don't have a plug and think you're going to make real money, you're probably playing yourself. I needed a plug, and my opportunity came one night when a particular out of town rapper asked me to take him and his crew to a strip club for some entertainment.

Where I come from, a lot of people hustle, a lot of people trap. In simple terms, trapping is selling drugs. It's what's going on in the area. Nature versus nurture. Survival of the fittest. Every long-term hustler is trying to get a plug. Somebody to give you a better price and give you what you need when you need it. There are really two sides to the trap game, people who have a plug (or possibly two or three) and people who don't. And there seems to be a clear difference in how life treats these individuals. People who have plugs seem to be lucky, and people who don't, well, the universe just seems to find a way to make sure they keep coming up short. When my rapper partner hit me up to kick it at the strip club, I stumbled upon my first plug.

I won't share the rapper's name, but we all went to Pin Ups in Decatur that night. He knew me from doing my one-two thing. He'd bought a little weed from me and knew I was dabbling in rap. He was probably around eight or nine deep. A few fellow rappers, some faces I kind of knew, and other people I had never seen before. I was by myself. I had my pistol on me, but I was by myself. I was driving my black BMW 750Li that night. I remember getting it cleaned up earlier that day.

When we pulled up to the club, I remember people checking out the whip. When we walked into the club, I remember people checking us out. Pin Ups had the vibe of most Atlanta strip clubs: main stage at the center, a few side stages, a couple of bars, flashing fluorescent blue and pink lights, a lot of tables. When we got in, we waited a few minutes for them to get our section together. The music was loud as hell, the bass made it impossible to hear anything. That's Atlanta strip club culture. It feels like you're actually in the speaker. You can dance if you want, throw money if you want, look at titties if you want. This was also the early 2000s, the height of Atlanta's strip club renaissance. Strip clubs were popping up everywhere, but some were longtime staples. Atlanta's history of gentlemen's clubs dates all the way back to the 1960s with Clermont Lounge being the oldest.

The rapper and his guys started congregating and smoking, getting into their mode. Dancers came over to our section and everything was vibing. The guys were not from Atlanta, so I was really trying to make sure they had a good time. Anytime you come to my city and hang with me, I'm going to make sure I host you properly.

One of the guys that stood out in their crew was this white dude. He wasn't really white, but he was white. I don't know how else to explain it. He pulled a half-bag of weed from his crotch and sat it on the table. He did it like it wasn't nothing, like he'd done that before. Folks started rolling up and smoking more. The white boy's role in the crew made perfect sense. He was in the perfect place with the perfect group. He supplied the weed, and the guys loved it. It's real convenient when the get-high supply guy is right there. You don't need to make any calls or run any errands.

While his role in the crew was to provide for everybody's recreational needs, I saw a business opportunity. *Something told me* to put this man in a business meeting he had no idea he'd be a part of.

"You got access to this shit?"

"Yeah, man, I get these shits all the time. I grow this shit. I do this," he told me in a strong West Coast accent.

"Damn, I would like to get a bag. I do my little hustling. What kind of numbers you got?"

"Aw man, for you, Tity Boi, I can do it for this." He wrote a number down on a napkin, and my first thought was *oh my*.

"When can I get one?"

"You can get one tomorrow. I got some shit down here."

We chopped it up, and he went into detail about how he lived out on the West Coast. He talked about how he grew his trees and the vibes out West. That was over twenty years ago, and me and him are still cool to this day.

Out of good faith, to show I wasn't on no bullshit, I met him the next day and bought my first bag. I immediately put that shit on the block, and people started going crazy. "Tity Boi got the belt." "You need to fuck with Tit, he got that strong." I knew I needed to keep it tough with white boy. He had that flavor.

Over time our relationship started to grow. He would fly me weed by the pound in his balls. I had been into real estate, so I had a couple of options on where to store it. My mom was a loan officer, and she had put me on the property game when I was growing up. From the time I was old enough to own property, I've had property. I ended up using a little apartment, but soon that became a problem. The work moved too fast, and I kept wanting more. It started getting crazy after a while. I was requesting bulk, twenty to thirty pounds at a time. I wanted to get more work in the city but had to figure out another way of storing and moving everything. It was too hot of a move to keep that much weed in an apartment I owned.

I decided on hotel rooms. On weekends, I'd get a room. I won't disclose the particular hotel but that became the move. White boy would send the bags to the hotel. It was wild that the hotel staff would just bring the packages right up to my room. They wouldn't question anything. Not what was inside the packages, or about why I was getting so many. They just delivered them to my room and stayed out the way.

I never missed a package. He started shipping me ten, then twenty bags at a time. The money was coming in, and *something told me* to use that to open up more doors. Not only was I hustling in College Park, but I was making moves in the Pittsburgh neighborhood of Atlanta as well. The ounces were going for about five or six hundred. Soon, I started to become one of them ones: I looked like it, I talked like it, I felt like it. Some niggas knew that I was trying to do my rap shit, but I started to get known for doing my trap shit. The more time that went by, the stronger me and white boy's relationship got.

The Pittsburgh apartments were like bricks. Each building had a circular driveway in front where folks would come in and out. I would park down the street, keep my pack in the car, and go and get zips (ounces) as needed. Business was going well, and white boy was making money too. But this isn't a story about the white boy, my first plug. This a story about my second plug. Because as soon as I started to feel like I was on top of the game, word of another plug started going around.

It didn't take long for me to come into contact with this new plug. One afternoon I found myself at the Burgh apartments getting work off. I had family near those apartments, so I hustled there often.

Like most of the life-changing things that've happened to me, that afternoon started off normal. I remember a woman showing some kids how to Double Dutch. That was about the only thing that stood out to me that day, initially. Mostly the afternoon was me chilling and people rolling up and getting work. I remember the constant routine of getting off work, and then checking back on the kids jump roping.

At one point, while I was watching the kids, I saw one of my niggas pacing the parking lot, holding his phone to his ear. Me and bruh went way back. We had a complicated friendship. I mean, we got along just fine, but we both sold drugs. He was one of the biggest hustlers.

He was the first drug dealer I knew who actually had a business card. Here's the thing, his business card was for lawn care service. How genius was that? Some people actually thought he cut grass. I mean, if we're being literal, he did. He cut the kind of grass that grows year-round. He was a real businessman. So, when I pulled up on him that afternoon, he didn't take his phone away from his ear.

"What's happening my nigga? What you got going on man?"

"You know me, just making moves," he responded, keeping his head on a swivel like he was expecting somebody.

"I hear that. Doing your thing, I see."

His phone stayed connected to his head that afternoon, and I soon understood why. Every few minutes after he would serve some work, he'd get on the phone and a car would pull up with more supply. I couldn't believe how he was running that shit. I thought my hustle had been efficient, but his system was a full-blown program: get weed, sell weed, immediately get more weed, rinse and repeat. When his plug would pull up with more work, I didn't recognize the car or the dude bringing it. *Something told me* to find out who was on the other end of his phone.

I started watching his phone, trying to make out a name, number, something. I was dead set on figuring it out. He was my biggest competition, and if there was a local plug that could supply that quickly, I needed to know who that motherfucker was.

"Say bruh, my phone dead, can I use your phone right quick to make a call?"

"Yeah man. Here you go." He casually handed me his phone and didn't even ask me to hurry up. That surprised me. My boy was slipping. It can be like that when business is going good. You can start to get way too comfortable. Before you know it, you're slipping and you're the last person to realize it.

After I got his phone, I started to walk away a little. I put all the information from his most recent calls into my phone. I knew the plug had to be the most recent number because that was the last person he was on the phone with. Even though I had that information, I knew it'd make more sense to call the plug from my nigga's phone. I had to keep everything consistent. I didn't want the person on the other end to suspect anything. The phone didn't even ring once before I heard a dude's voice on the other end:

"What you need?"

"What's up? Man, this Slim."

"This who?"

"Slim from the apartments, nigga. Bring me two of them bags too."

"Oh, okay. I got you. Here I come."

It was that easy. That was all it took. He asked zero questions. He trusted the number and knew I had to be good for it. And I was. I gave my nigga his phone back, and the plug came to the apartments fifteen or twenty minutes later. He served my nigga two zips and served me two. I knew my nigga was wondering how I got the plug, but I just acted like I knew him. I finessed it just like people do me when they walk up to me acting like they've known me forever: "What's up 2 Chainz." I just acted like we knew each other, like we went to school together.

There was no reason for hanging out any longer at the Burgh apartments. I'd gotten everything I was supposed to get that day. Easy play. That was the day I ran into a new plug, my second plug, a local plug. I didn't need white boy shipping me work from the West anymore. I now had immediate weed access. That was all I needed.

My name was already Teflon in the streets, and I already had more clients than I could supply. That would no longer be a problem. Me and my new plug hit it off and ended up building the best relationship. He one of them ones in the city of Atlanta. I'm not going to put his name out there, but we grew up and made money in the city of Atlanta. Millions.

That had always been the thing about me. While I shared circles with a lot of players who had similar interests, none of them had my nature. None of them was made like me, even though we walked the same streets. I learned that in college. I preferred being in the streets but learned I was of a different design. People gravitated toward me. All I needed was to get in the right room with the right people and everything else was simple. In due time, this would apply to my music career, too.

Nothing about finding my first two plugs was luck. It was a God thing. I created my luck.

Experimental psychologist Richard Wiseman spent a decade studying both lucky and unlucky people. He found that there are four principles separating lucky people from unlucky. One of those principles, Principle Two, he calls "Listening to Lucky Hunches." He said: "Lucky people make effective decisions by listening to their intuition and gut feelings. In addition, they take steps to actively boost their intuitive abilities by, for example, meditating and clearing their mind of other thoughts."

I hadn't started meditating yet, but my intuitive voice led to no more cross-country bags from white boy. *Something told me* to "jump." And I just had to ask myself how high, because I knew I could reach that goal.

My first two plugs changed my life. They helped me

get my first house, the house I bought for my mom. That house was bought off the bag. Working with a local plug completely opened up Atlanta. I was able to get work faster, and that allowed me to serve more of the city.

My second plug ended up supplying me with a new gas he called Irene. I introduced her to Atlanta. Irene and the city made an immediate love connection. She was a stronger gas that created a more intense high. Irene changed everything. I started making real money. But this wasn't a story about Irene. And it wasn't a story about my second plug. This was a story on how I used my mind to meet someone who could help facilitate the work that I needed.

V

THE WHOLE FOUNDATION SHAKING

Me and mama used to trap out the same house . . .
Me and mama got busted at the same time
"Proud"

Everything requires a solid foundation. The first part of building a lasting home is the kind of soil you use before you start building that thing. A house needs steel rods before you lay the concrete down. Then once you start building, it doesn't matter how much money you put into the light fixtures or that pretty little kitchen island if the foundation is quicksand.

I remember folks from around my way having solid hustle ideas without solid foundations. I would listen to their hustle play and realize the errors of their foundation from the jump. Imagine opening up your own beauty salon without anyone to manage it. Or maybe you think you're going to run it yourself, but you don't have any entrepreneurial experience.

Our personal foundation, as people, begins long before we drive our first car, or ask someone to the prom. It starts when we're growing up, and that voice is somewhere itching in our ears, trying to remind us of the foundation we're built on and which direction to move toward. Sometimes I think about the things I experienced growing up, and I'm thankful my children will never have to experience that. They will, however, face obstacles I never had to experience and might not even understand.

When I think about foundation, I think about being grounded—what's needed to build something sustainable from the ground up. You need a really strong foundation. Now, that can be in family, business, or whatever you deal with. In this case, I'm talking about the foundation of a house. I have been in three or four drug busts, and they all happened at home, and they were all with my family.

I started selling packs with my mom at a young age. Yes, with my mom. I was young, but my maturity level was much older. Maybe it was because of my pops and my mom. I was really understanding life at an early age. Maybe it was God, or trapping, or both, but I always stayed within my own frequency. I always preferred the frequency of older people, so I always hung out with people much older than me. My pops sold work, so I started selling packs with my mom around twelve. Selling packs just seemed to be the family business, and it felt as natural as going to school.

Thank God I've never been in any home invasions. But I have been in my share of police busts. A few happened when I was young. The first happened at the first house me, my mama, and pops lived at. It was around Christmastime because I remember the tree and Christmas lights blinking. I remember the layout of the house. When you walked in, my parents' bedroom was on the left, and my bedroom was across the hall from theirs on the right. I had to leave my door open unless they closed it. This was much different from how my kids will now go into their room and close the door. I couldn't do that. If they were having company, they'd close my door, but otherwise, I had to leave it open.

The whole situation started with my pops running in like he was being chased. Back then, my pops had the coolest stash spot in the world. The bathroom mirror took up the whole wall above our sink. The mirror had these little plastic clips on the side that you could remove to take down the mirror. My pops would hit those clips with a power drill, *ziit, ziit, ziit*. This was in the eighties, and back then, a power drill was like a new technology. Him owning a power drill was another thing that made him the man in our neighborhood. He would take the mirror down, and there was a hole behind it where he kept his pounds of weed.

Anytime I would hear that sound back then (*ziit, ziit, ziit*), I knew what was going down. He was either dumping some weed in or taking some out. Even when I hear that sound now, I'm thrown right back into that house, right back into those moments.

The night of the first bust, I heard my pops run into the house out of breath. It was around three in the morning, and I had been sleeping. Me hearing him running in loud started to wake me up, and I really woke up once I heard him yelling my mama's name: "Jeanette, Jeanette, I think they're about to hit the house."

Immediately after he said that, I heard the familiar

drill sound, *ziit, ziit, ziit*. At the time, I was only around four or five, but I knew what was going on. The Christmas tree was so bright that night, just lighting up the whole house, while folks were running around screaming. The first thing we heard the police say was, "Come out, and if you don't, we're going to take a bulldozer and knock this whole house down." Then, shortly after, we started hearing the battering ram, and the whole foundation of the house started shaking. Then, motherfuckers just started coming inside.

From my adult perspective, I realize that the police must've followed him from a deal, or what we call a play. When the police came through the door, they told my pops to freeze and "drop that damn weapon." My pops was an outlaw but not crazy enough to have a pistol or anything like that in his hand. He did still have the drill in his hand. And they had their flashlights and weapons pointed at him.

I'm not sure I'll ever understand what happened next or why my pops proceeded to do what he did. But he started to seriously pop off, behaving like he had a death wish. He grabbed the hand of one of the officers who was holding a gun and placed the gun to his own head: "Shit, kill me. Go ahead and kill me. Gone and do it. If you gone kill me, just gone and do it."

I had my head down on the bed. My pops started to get beat with guns and flashlights. I closed my eyes. They started putting my parents in handcuffs, but at some point, before we all left the house, either my pops or mom filled my jeans with something.

By the time we got outside, I found out that my Doberman, Toom Toom, had been killed by the cops. I never saw my dog, but I knew he was dead, and my pops believed the cops did it. That devastated me more than all the chaos. Toom Toom was my dog. My motherfucking dog, and my best friend.

My pops had put me on game back then on how to keep police dogs from being able to sense dope. He'd always keep lime and pepper laid out around the house. He told me it'd keep the police dogs sneezing and they wouldn't be able to smell nothing, both inside and outside. My pops later told me the lime and pepper pissed off the cops who showed up that night. They asked my pops, "Epps, what the fuck are you trying to do to our dogs?" I don't know if that made them hurt Toom Toom, or if they thought he was a threat. I just know Toom Toom died during that bust, and I know I'm still mad about that shit.

Both my parents went to jail that night. I went to my grandma's house. Once I got there, I found out what had been stuffed in my jeans. A few family members took me to the bathroom and started stripping me down. At first, I started pushing them off me because I didn't understand why they were taking my clothes off. My aunt and them started taking packs off me. I guess my mom had given me a hug or something before we separated and ended up putting packs in my Jordache jeans. I remember their faces shining like them damn Christmas lights when they started pulling drugs out of every pocket.

The second drug bust happened when I was in seventh grade. I went to Gresham Park Elementary School, but stayed in the Pittsburgh neighborhood with my mom and her boyfriend. They drove me to Decatur every day for school. At the time, my mom's boyfriend had his campaign going on. He had one of them horse-and-carriage setups in

Atlanta. You know the folks who park a horse attached to a carriage on the side of the road waiting to see if anybody want a ride around the city? He was one of them and actually one of the first ones doing that in Atlanta.

He had a solid business that was actually profitable. But he had bricks, too. I wouldn't call the horse-carriage business a coverup, but he made his real money a different way. Him and my mom both knew that I liked nice things. They both knew I was a hustler and into clothes and fashion (I'd been into fashion my whole life). In a move to support me and my fashion sense, they'd appointed me to sell nicks. Small five-dollar sacks.

The play was simple: I'd sit up in one of our house windows that wasn't too high off the ground but high enough so people couldn't fuck with me. People would come and give me money, and I would give them drugs. For every fifty dollars I made, I probably only ended up with twenty. But that was cool with me. I'd make my twenty and take it to the candy lady. My pockets stayed full of Airheads, Funyuns, and Faygo drinks.

It didn't take long for the police to come and see us. I had been working the window play for about two weeks when one night, while I was sitting in the window, I saw nine dark-colored Ford Tauruses lined up down the street. There was something about how synchronized they were. *Something told me* they were there for us. But I didn't say anything. I didn't move.

Officers started getting out of the cars, and the first thing they did was approach my granddaddy's Cadillac in our driveway. I don't know why my mom had my granddaddy's Cadillac at the time. It was brown, and it was clean. They opened all the doors and searched the car.

They didn't spend much time in the car. Maybe they didn't find anything. I'll never know. I do know they moved to our back door next, and without any word or warning, they started hitting that motherfucker. *Boom. Boom.* The whole house started shaking, even the foundation. A familiar motion.

I started freaking out because I was stuck, and that probably was the only time in my life I've ever been stuck. We thought we had a super-secure door until it started getting hit with that big-ass battering ram. *Boom.* There was a group of them hitting the door. *Boom.* It probably took three tries before the door finally buckled. I could hear it all happening from my room.

I stared out the window praying it was all a dream. I was the first person to see them. I saw them before they'd gotten into the yard. I told myself maybe it wasn't real. It all seemed too cinematic, too scripted. I felt like I was there but not there. And I was only twelve. I was a child. As the late, great Notorious B.I.G. once said, "It was all a dream," until I heard my mom scream from the other room. A familiar sound. Then everything got too real.

"Ty, do whatever they tell you to do. You hear me son?" she shouted from the other room.

There were other aggressive voices, but I couldn't make out what they were saying. I knew we were in trouble. Shit, I knew *I* was in trouble. I had been sitting in the window selling five-dollar nickel bags in plain sight. At the time we had a maid. Wait, let me explain. She was a J (junkie) that we hired to keep our house clean. She was a respectable addict. At the time she was almost like family and had a way of protecting me. I was tall for only twelve. I was the tallest person in the seventh grade. I wasn't quite six feet, but I was close enough. To the police I was tall, Black, and looked a lot older than I was. We know how this goes, right? Not to mention, my demeanor and the way I carried myself didn't appear to be adolescent at all. So, when they made their way through our house, I knew I'd be fair game just like everybody else.

When the police finally got to the living room, *something told me* not to move. To just stay still like I had been. I'd thought about jumping out the window, but I didn't. The maid told them, "He's just a baby. He's just a kid." They immediately laid me down and started patting me down. I didn't say anything. I remember them being gentler with the maid. Maybe because she was a woman. I'm not sure. They weren't gentle with me, though. Even though she had told them I was a kid, they didn't seem to give a fuck. And even though I was quiet and complied, that didn't seem to be enough.

My mama and her boyfriend ended up going to jail. They put neon handcuffs on my mom and her boyfriend and took them away. My pops was already in jail, so they needed to do something with me before DFCS (Georgia Department of Human Services Division of Family & Children Services) got involved.

I ended up calling one of my favorite girl cousins who would do anything for me. She was really like my favorite cousin. I ended up staying with her in Decatur for a while until my mama got some things together. Thankfully, her boyfriend took the rap, so my mama didn't stay in jail long. But even when she got out, I continued to stay with my cousin for a while.

I felt really bad for a long time because I wasn't able to warn them. I was the one who saw the Tauruses lined up. I saw them checking the Cadillac in the driveway. I saw them heading for our back door and never warned anybody. I was the lookout and didn't do my job. I felt like I failed my family.

I know that a lot of people didn't have to go through what I went through growing up. These memories stay with me until this day. I'm thankful for all the times *something told me* to be still when I came face-to-face with the police. I'm thankful I listened to my intuition. I'm happy to never know what other outcomes there could've been had I not listened.

When I stayed with my cousin in Decatur, I was doing my thing. I was hustling. Rest in peace Big Ken, who gave me my first fifty-dollar slab of crack to hold. I had been doing the weed thing, but I got my first fifty-dollar slab from Big Ken in Countryside Apartments. Rest in peace to the legend. A for real legend in the game.

I ended up breaking that fifty-dollar slab down into twelve rocks that I sold at ten dollars apiece. What a business hustle. I had spent fifty, and after cutting everything up, came out seventy dollars ahead. After I sold the one-twenty, I used the residual to get more work from Big Ken. See, the thing I knew about selling crack was that I'd never use it.

Unlike weed, I didn't need to worry about getting high off my own supply. I repeated the process of breaking fifty-dollar slabs down to twelve rocks until I was able to buy my first pair of Jordans. After that, I didn't turn around, I never looked back. I was really out there.

I was staying at my cousin's house, but I was kind of violating. I was fucking girls and trapping while my cousin was at work. I was doing the most, and my cousin had gotten tired of my shit. I ended up moving back with my mom who at the time was staying in College Park, on Riverdale Road. This was how I even started going to North Clayton and meeting a bunch of new friends. Around the middle of ninth grade, I met some real hustlers who were like-minded like me.

I was making new friends, and so was my mom, who started dating a new nigga that hustled. It was like anywhere she went, she'd find a nigga who hustled. Her new nigga sold dope. I can't say I ever really fucked with the nigga. I can't even remember his name, but he'd be the reason I experienced my third drug bust.

I was fourteen, lying on my air mattress sleeping, and once again, around two or three in the morning, a loud commotion woke me up. I sat up and heard my mama's boyfriend running to the bathroom. Groundhog Day. He was panicking and flushing the toilet repeatedly.

I stood up and started walking toward the bathroom, but before I could make it there, the police ran into our apartment. The whole foundation started to shake. I wasn't sure what to do, but I had been through it before. I didn't need to ask any questions. I don't know if in that moment I actually thought about the other incidents.

Either way, looking back now, I know my body remembered because I froze. Just like I had two years prior. And while I stood there frozen, I remembered what was beside the air mattress. Back then, I had this bedtime routine. Every night before I went to sleep, I would eat cookies with milk. Every single night. It was one of my innocent pleasures that nobody outside my house knew about. On that night, I had my routine cookies and milk before resting my eyes. Only that night, I ended up balling up around ten crack rock dimes in a napkin and placing it in the empty red milk cup.

"I have to pee," I told the cops as soon as they saw me standing in the hallway. I was spooked and didn't know how else to keep them away from my bedroom. They had already gotten a hold of my mama's boyfriend. That nigga was cooked.

"You can pee, but you have to leave the door open." They wanted to watch me. They wanted to watch me pee. Their request was not only awkward but embarrassing. I had no clue what was going on. I pulled it out and started trying to pee. They stood there and watched. The problem was that no pee was coming out, and the harder I tried, the less likely it seemed I'd actually pee. I was nervous as fuck.

The two cops stayed watching. I imagined they wanted to see if I would try to flush work like my mama's boyfriend did. They kept on watching me and watched while no pee came out. The irony was that I actually had to pee but couldn't with them watching. Even to this day, it's hard for me to pee without privacy. One of the cops started smiling. "Uh huh. I thought you had to pee man." He was borderline laughing, mocking me, until I finally peed.

After I finished, they sent me into the hallway. From the hallway I could see into my bedroom. I could see my unmade air mattress and the red milk cup. They went to my bedroom and started tearing shit up. They flipped the air mattress and searched the floor, my drawers, and the closet. My room was small, so it didn't take them long to look through everything. They weren't finding anything. I heard my mom and her boyfriend being taken out of the house. I sat and watched the cops the way they had watched me. I had been trying to pee but couldn't, and they had been trying to find dope but couldn't. We were even.

After not finding anything, they seemed to be done with my room. I finally breathed a little. But right after, one of the cops, an Asian dude wearing Hi-Tec boots, accidentally kicked my milk cup over. I remember he was Asian only because he was the only one not wearing a ski mask. A sack of crack fell out of the cup onto the floor. My heart fell out my chest and right onto the floor with it.

"Oh, look what we got here."

They took my mama and her boyfriend to jail. I had to get somebody to come and get me again.

I went back to our apartment a week or two later, and it had been ransacked by people in the neighborhood. People in the neighborhood knew our apartment had been busted, so they came through and took everything: clothes, TVs, everything.

There was no need for me to go back to that house, so I had to figure things out on my own. I started staying with my homeboy and his family until my mom got out and got herself together again. My pops was already incarcerated at the time, so he wasn't around to save me.

My homeboy I was staying with ended up not going to school as often as I did. I was at school one Wednesday, and folks started telling me that the principal was looking for me. I was confused because I hadn't been doing anything. I ended up finding out that a letter had been sent to the apartment saying I needed to go to court for the work the police had found. Since I never saw the letter, I never went to court. Since I never went to court, they ended up issuing a warrant.

They came to get me out of school that day, in the tenth grade, and that's when I went to juvenile detention. That's when I started to tighten up my basketball skills, in juvenile detention. I became a hoop star in Juve. Their Kobe Bryant. A trap nigga. Crossing niggas over, gliding through the air in boxer shorts worn backwards so my dick wouldn't fall out.

I don't want to preach, but I know these experiences have affected my family's foundation. Me and mom have needed to work through a lot to be in the headspace we're in today. We still have a ways to go, but we'll get there.

VI

WALKING IN MY PURPOSE

In the early 2000s, I was doing my hustling thing. And throughout that time I would meet different individuals in the music industry. Back then, Ludacris and a guy by the name Poon Daddy worked on the radio here in Atlanta. Any time entertainers came into town and got on the radio, they would call me and tell me to come through, especially if the entertainer smoked cannabis. Providing cannabis was my lane.

This one time, Diddy was in town. There was a party at a club called Visions. I remember BMF being there. It was going down. I remember them spending big that night. At the time, I was one foot in and one foot out. Trying to do my rap thing but doing my trap thing. I was trying to really take the rap thing full-fledged serious. It was a Tuesday night and I was with Poon. Since he was familiar with Diddy, we approached him in the club.

I'll never forget Poon telling Diddy like, "Yo man, I got an artist you might be interested in." Diddy was like, "I'm actually looking. I'm looking for like the next HOV. Some down south niggas with swag and charisma, so to speak."

Poon pointed to me and said, "Boy, this your man. This the man for the job."

Diddy was with it. "Alright. This weekend the NBA All-Star game is in Philadelphia. Meet me up there. You know what I'm saying? Bring some music, let's hang out."

A couple of days went by, and I found myself out looking to get some gas, some weed. A homie of mine on the Southside had some, but I thought it was short, meaning it didn't have all the grams to it. I wanted some weed to take with me to Philadelphia the next day, so I ended up going to these apartments in Pittsburgh, where I had been trapping at, making juggs, making plays, to see what kind of gas they had there.

When I got there, there was a line of dudes near the front area. My wife Kesha was driving, and Poon was in the back seat. So, I'm going through, smelling packs of weed. I remember looking at this one dude in particular. And I could tell he was up to something. He was like pointing with his eyes, trying to get me to look to the side. Then, out of nowhere, a different guy pointed a gun dead at my chest.

Ironically, a couple of weeks before this, my homeboy Goat was set to go to prison. Before he went in, he had a .38 pistol he wanted to sell. For some reason, that pistol stuck in my memory. I remembered that pistol after Goat showed it to me. I still remember that pistol today. I knew the grip, size, and color. The pistol that the guy pointed into my chest in the Pittsburgh apartments reminded me of that pistol. I can't say for sure, but damn, it looked just like the pistol Goat was trying to sell.

I swiped the pistol down, and it went off. Shot me right in my ankle. I had on some Timberlands, and it shot me right in my laces. Everything happened so fast. I remember my foot being on fire.

People started dispersing, you know, going different ways. There was a billboard in the plaza in Pittsburgh that had Luda, I-20, Fate, and Shondrae on it. The whole DTP crew. I remember seeing it on my way in. I had been hanging with those dudes in DTP trying to get my rap thing on, and now some jealous ass niggas were trying to get in the way of my purpose. They were trying to disrupt my momentum. There was no doubt about it. I had been shot, and I had a flight to meet with Diddy the very next day.

Something told me not to even go over to the apartments, because I was getting presented with weed where I was, but I really just wanted to ride out. You know what I'm saying? Don't ask me why. Sometimes a person might just want to get in the streets, get some fresh air. Even though *something told me* not to go over there, I never expected to get shot. When I limped back to the car, Kesha and Poon was asking me what happened. "That nigga shot me, shawty," was all I could say, "Nigga really shot me."

My first reaction was to find something to calm me down. I needed something to distract me from the pain. I needed to smoke. I needed a blunt. We stopped at the gas station to get a blunt. Poon ended up rolling me one of the nastiest blunts I'd ever seen. Man, it was just a nasty, fat, sloppy ass blunt. He just kind of threw that shit together. It didn't matter though. I was still hitting that motherfucker on our way to Grady Memorial Hospital. Shit, Grady was right around the corner from the Pittsburgh apartments.

When we pulled up, they came out with the wheelchair. Once I got inside, the people helping me asked if I had been smoking because I was bleeding a lot. I was like, bleeding extra. Apparently, smoking weed thins your blood somehow and you bleed more. I found out that night.

Grady was bunking that night. It was crazy packed. They didn't have any rooms available, so I had to sit in the hallway. Keep in mind, my flight was at like seven in the morning. Nothing was going to keep me from making it. I didn't know nothing about changing flights or redirecting anything; I just knew that I was making that damn flight. If you can't tell by now, I'm a spiritually based individual. The chaos I was experiencing just seemed like a sign from God. Don't they say we experience our hardest lessons before our biggest blessings? I felt like God was telling me to get out the streets and take the music more seriously. I tried to focus on putting forth that good energy, making silent promises to stay straight, keep in my lane going forward, as long as I got on that flight.

I remember asking the nurse what the doctor could do about my foot. I didn't have time to just be sitting there. I had a flight to catch. They ended up cleaning my wound with some solution and wrapping it in an Ace bandage. The bullet was still in me, and I was still very much bleeding. They gave me clear instructions: *take this, make sure you clean the wound four or five times a day, change the wrap, blah, blah, blah.*

All of this happened in the hospital hallway. I never even got a chance to go see a doctor. I just left, went straight to the airport, and jumped on the flight. I sat in an exit row seat. The nurses had told me to keep my foot elevated but that couldn't happen on a plane. I had never been shot before, and my adrenaline was through the roof.

The higher the plane elevated, the more my foot throbbed. Shit, my whole leg started throbbing, man. It was almost like it had a pulse. My foot was swelling and bleeding profusely through the bandage. People probably noticed. I was growing concerned. I found myself questioning if I had made the right decision to hop on the flight without proper medical attention. At the same time, I believed my meeting with Diddy would go well. I saw my future clearly. I had vision.

We eventually made it to Philly, and I cleaned myself up. We went over to the hotel Diddy was staying at. Me, Poon, and Shondrae. Shondrae was and is a bona fide music producer. There was security down in the middle of the hall near Diddy's room. This was also around the time when Fonzworth Bentley was around, and they let us in.

Inside the room was Diddy, Bentley, and I want to say that maybe Diddy's kid Justin was there. He was just a kid then. When we walked into the room, Diddy noticed I was on crutches. He had just seen me like three days ago, so he was a little shocked. He looked at my foot and then at me and asked, "Yo, what happened to you?"

All I could say was, "I got shot last night."

"Yo, you need to move."

I agreed with him and said, "That's why I'm right here." Once again, my internal compass knew it was a sign. *Something telling me* I need to be right here with you, man, trying to figure this out.

The meeting became like a vibe session for educational purposes. We talked about a lot of things and got to know each other. He asked me who my influences were. I mentioned everyone from Outkast, to UGK, to Three Six Mafia. We went on to have a long conversation about 8Ball & MJG and their influence on the South. I remember Bentley being really excited during that conversation. We talked about how even though 8Ball & MJG were from Memphis, they still had a huge impact on Atlanta music and culture. Bentley was a cool dude, too. I had already known he was from Atlanta, but that day I found out that he was from the Southside.

I learned and grew a lot that day, but I didn't sign with Diddy. This was before I became 2 Chainz. I was still Tity Boi. Not too long afterward, Diddy ended up creating Bad Boy South. He signed 8Ball & MJG. Now that I think about it, and our conversations in the hotel room that day, I might've had something to do with them getting signed. And guess who ended up doing a good amount of the production on 8Ball & MJG's Bad Boy South project? Shondrae! Whose producer name is Bangladesh.

A few years after that I started getting piped up and made a name for myself, 2 Chainz. I saw Diddy at a show in LA. Man, it was packed. I remember Diddy pulling up on me like, "Tity Boi! Remember you came to my room after you got shot. Boy, you came a long way." I said, "Boy, you remember that was me?"

I was surprised. Sometimes people will walk up on me, and tell me, "Ah, man, I booked you in 2013," but I don't always remember them because I meet so many people. I was never going to remind Diddy that I was the guy that came to his room, foot bleeding through the bandages, on crutches. But once he mentioned our meeting, it gave me an emotion I can't explain. I had come a long way, but I had envisioned everything all along. You know what I'm saying?

The Bahamian teacher and minster, Dr. Myles Munroe once said about vision: "Vison should be out of reach but never out of sight. It's important for you to pursue something that you haven't done and that's not easy to do either. All visions from God are very difficult to pursue. They demand His assistance, and so it's critical for you as a person to remember that visions from God are always bigger than your capacity as a human by yourself. It's important to understand that vision is to see the future from the present. To stand on the porch of the present and see the future vision."

I have always stood on the porch of the present and manifested my future. I was standing there when my foot was bloody on the way to Grady. I was on that porch when I took that flight to Philly and my leg was killing me. And even when I rocked out the show in LA to a packed house with Diddy watching, I was still on that porch. I knew even then I had higher places to go. That I was supposed to keep walking in my purpose. That one day I'd write a book like this. That my purpose will always have a higher purpose.

VII

IS THAT JD AND JAY-Z ON THREE-WAY?

If I trace myself back, I have always been curious about time and timing. One thing about the industry is that you can be in the right place at the right time. You can be at the right place at the wrong time. You can be at the wrong place at the wrong time. You can also be at the wrong place at the right time. Everything happens the way it should. But you have to put thought into the decisions you make and try and find the reason for every outcome.

Think about the 2004 movie *The Butterfly Effect* with Ashton Kutcher, in which his character is able to travel back in time to prevent certain things from happening, but every time he returns to the present, something different is fucked-up. No matter what he does to try and create the perfect scenario, it always has a negative impact on something else.

In a 2023 *Forbes* article titled "A Psychologist Makes Sense of the 'Butterfly Effect' in Relationships," psychologist Mark Travers breaks down "three manifestations of the butterfly effect in relationships and strategies to navigate its impact." The three he lists are "Emotional Echoes," "Communication: The Domino Effect," and "Decisions Ripple."

Everything happens the way it should because if you change one thing, it'll have a significant impact on everything else. In the "Decisions Ripple" section, Travers writes, "Every decision, no matter how trivial, shapes the trajectory of our lives and the course of our connections ever so slightly. The butterfly effect is particularly evident in choices related to time, priorities and commitments, impacting relationships inadvertently."

It's important to place a lot of thought into every decision, especially big decisions. Think about the vibrational effects they could have on everything else in your life or the people you're close with. To explain the dramatic, unexpected effects of small things that might not seem connected but are, in the 1960s mathmatician and meteorologist Edward Lorenz used the example of a butterfly flapping its wings in Brazil causing a tornado in Texas.

I think about timing and the butterfly effect when I think about my journey in the music industry. Everything has happened at the time it was supposed to and how it was supposed to. I've placed a lot of thought into every industry decision I've made. The industry can be forgiving, but it also can turn against you. One day you can be loved by everybody, and the next some of your personal business can get out that has nothing to do with anybody or anything. Popular opinion has a way of swaying judgment and how people feel about you.

There are more followers than leaders, right? That's just how it goes. Your few leaders will determine which way things are supposed to go, and your followers will follow. I've learned the importance of having a strong moral compass and to ensure I lead with integrity in everything I do. The industry doesn't make this easy. This is why there aren't many people with lengthy careers. There haven't been many people who've been able to say "I'm not going to be able to do it" because of the possible ramifications associated with saying no. It's hard for most people.

Saying something as simple as "I'm not going to be able to show up," or "I can't make it," is hard for most people in the industry. Somebody could know deep down in their spirit that a certain move will have a lasting negative effect on their career but may still agree to do it because the money is there, or they don't want to let a certain person down.

A lot of people in the industry lack integrity. Hell, a lot of people in life lack integrity.

A lot of people don't possess a firm moral base, something they can turn to or refer to when they find themselves in potentially compromising situations. We spend our lives going through many trials and errors, discovering what does and doesn't work for us. We also spend our lives witnessing how certain decisions made by others have impacted them over time: "I watched X make that decision and in the short term it worked out for them, but in the long term it derailed their career."

We inadvertently begin our cause-and-effect research when we're just kids. Something might've happened on the grade-school playground that's shaped who we are today. Character building begins way before we even understand what character is.

My moral compass started forming probably before

grade school. My parents instilled character in me from the moment I could speak and understand. My pops's teachings have actually become some of the voices in my head. I can actually hear old guidance in his actual tone of voice. The decisions we make tally up over time and create a register for us to refer to when we find ourselves needing to make hard decisions. Learning how past decisions have affected us and the people around us helps to locate what integrity is.

We might say to ourselves, "Even though this isn't grade school and I'm a grown adult now, the spirit of this situation feels like the spirit of a situation I experienced in fifth grade. And in that situation, I chose option A, which got me suspended and somebody got hurt. This time I'm going to take another path." God has made us all differently, so the decisions we make in these situations are not necessarily a commentary on the people surrounding the situation. Meaning, people aren't always out trying to do you wrong. It's simply knowledge of the self and knowing what works for each of us individually.

In addition to having integrity, we all possess the intuitive voice that should be the first thing we reference when making tough decisions. When something is telling you that a situation is bad for you, you should listen to that voice. One thing I know is that no matter what has happened or what will happen in my career, I'm able to live with it because I've listened to my inner voice (which is God to me) and have led a life of integrity. This is why I can walk around the city of Atlanta without security when I choose to.

If you're winning with a lack of integrity, as soon as you start losing, people kind of cheer for that. I call it "going down the ladder." When you're going up the ladder, you pass people. And when you pass people, you might start talking shit the whole time you're stepping on them. You find yourself saying shit like "Watch out," or "It's my turn." I've always known there to be a more elegant way to move up the ladder, but some people can't help themselves. It's so enticing when you hot to just tell people to get the hell out the way, or constantly remind them of how much they're not fucking with you. But when your ass come back down, and pass somebody you shitted on, that person probably won't have a hand for you. And I swear I understand all sides.

When you've never had anything and didn't think you could get to a certain spot, man, it's something about shitting on people that can make us feel good. But doing that can, and most likely will, bite you in the ass.

As far as the industry, it's what Hov (Jay-Z) once said, "Show 'em how to move in a room full of vultures." You have alcohol, you have drugs period, you have vacation, you have stimulation, and you got motivation.

One night in 2011 I received a phone call from my brother, the maestro songwriter, executive producer, entrepreneur, rapper, and studio trapper Jermaine Dupri (JD). Jermaine was raised in Atlanta, so that's how we knew each other. At the time I had gone cold turkey from selling bags. I'd had enough of that lane. It can only take you so far, as we all know. Dead or in jail is how they say it always ends up, and I never wanted to be in nobody's grave or back in nobody's cage.

I had invested all my energy into rapping and beats. I had already been rapping for some time but was finally rapping rapping full-time. Damn near every night I was either on somebody's stage or in somebody's studio. I had a great rhythm going. The music was becoming an addiction.

It's hard to describe how it feels when something begins feeling like a calling. Well, maybe I can try. It's like falling in love. You know how it is when you're falling in love, right? There's the emotional part when your insides start acting all crazy. Then there's the physical part when you always wanting to be around that person no matter what you got going on. Then there's the most important part, the spiritual part. That gut feeling or inner voice that tells you, even in your sleep, *That's the one.* Making music was starting to feel that way. Every day and night that I made music, I kept hearing my inner voice saying to me, *That's the one.*

I had been stepping into my calling and started becoming more recognized in Atlanta. Getting a call from JD was nothing new, we'd been cool from the music scene. I had been running in the same circles as a lot of major players. My music and how I moved was becoming well respected.

When I answered the phone that night, I didn't expect JD to say, "Hov is feeling your work and wants to speak with you about a potential record deal. I'm going to bring him in this phone call on three-way if that's cool?" Hell yeah that was cool with me. Hov had long established himself as a giant among giants in not only the rap industry but music in general and popular culture. Me and Hov had brushed shoulders from time to time but hadn't had any real conversations. There had always been mutual respect, but we didn't really know each other.

JD added Hov to the call and the three of us started talking. It was mostly me and Hov singing each other's praises and discussing how excited we were to possibly work together. It felt like a dream proposition. Hov had been at the top, and that's exactly where I was headed. JD played middleman during the conversation and, the whole time, the vibes were incredible.

We had a lot in common. From our background in trapping to our charismatic demeanors. Everything seemed right and for a minute, I thought I might be signing a deal. We eventually moved on to discussing a time and date to meet and maybe iron out the details of what a deal could look like.

This was my time. I was in the right place at the right time about to sign the right deal. After ironing out the details of the trip, I ended up mentioning I'd need two flights: one for me, and one for my dog Tek. Tek had been a deejay and he was my manager at the time. He was one of the first people to believe in me. I'll never forget in one of our first conversations him telling me, "Man you a star." I responded by saying "duh" because it was something I had already known. And even though I had already known I was a star, him telling me meant a lot.

By 2011, me and Tek had been through a lot, and I never imagined a situation where we wouldn't eat together. If not for Tek rocking with me and believing in me, Hov wouldn't had even known who I was.

When I told Hov I needed two flights, he didn't seem to understand why I wanted to bring my deejay to the meeting. At that time my dog went by DJ Tek. I tried explaining that Tek was more than just my manager, we were a package, true brothers. I found myself in one of those difficult situations.

Long story short, it didn't end up being a good fit. While it would've been amazing to work with Hov and being connected with his superstardom could've rocketed my career, it would've meant leaving my dog behind. Loyalty has always been an important aspect of how I understand my integrity. My moral compass. Who I am as a soul.

When I think about all the people who could've just left me behind coming up but didn't, I think about how their loyalty shaped me. I also had my inner voice assuring me, *There will be other opportunities for you to get the right deal at the right time, exactly how YOU want.* As much as I had and still have great respect for both JD and Jay-Z, I couldn't leave my dog behind. I had to pass on the meeting. After that incident, I made Tek remove the DJ from his name.

I know I made the right decision because of the way everything has turned out for me. I not only have the life I'm supposed to have but the life I want. I think about the butterfly effect and how my life might've turned out had I taken the deal. What if I took the deal and my disloyalty to my brother Tek ruined our relationship, or we never became the kind of brothers we are now? I've made some classic albums and songs that would've never happened because I would've been under a different label. What if the music industry never got "I'm Different" or "Watch Out"? Man, that would have been a tragedy.

Imagine if that other life had different demands pulling me away from becoming the kind of family man I've grown into. My integrity has always come first, and it has always worked for me. I don't live a life of regrets because I understand my voice has been guiding me this entire time, and I've been listening. Just like I was on three-way with JD and Jay-Z, I'm constantly on three-way with God and those ancestors that look out for me.

VIII

DOS CADENAS

Me llama Dos Cadenas, baby, buenas noches

"Bad Choices"

I was signed to Def Jam in the early 2000s as a group through Ludacris's Disturbing Tha Peace (DTP) label. Me and my homeboy Dolla Boy had a group called Playaz Circle. We had a nice little thing going on. My rap name was still Tity Boi at the time. I knew some people over at Def Jam. Some of the people over there I liked, some I didn't. It was the same as it is with anyplace. You're not always going to like everybody, and not everybody is always going to like you. I've always been cool with that.

Me and Dolla were childhood friends and had been putting work into the rap game for a minute. As Playaz Circle we had some hits, including "Duffle Bag Boy," which featured Wayne (Lil Wayne). That song actually peaked at fifteen on the *Billboard* Hot 100 and eventually went platinum.

The kind of exposure that song created allowed me a more intimate look into the music business and an opportunity to see its inner workings. I've always been a curious businessman before anything. If I'm going to be involved in something, I need to know how everything works and what everybody does; I'm talking down to the custodians. People will try to take advantage of you or talk over you if they believe you don't know what's going on. I have not and will not ever allow myself to be naïve in any situation I'm working in.

Performing "Duffle Bag Boy" allowed me the opportunity to polish my stage presence and showmanship. It was a time of growth for me. I started to understand my power as an artist and an individual, and the ways I can change a room. I've always been a leader, and being around Chris (Ludacris) and Wayne started to show me that I could do things on my own. I had known I was a star but tightening up my stage show started to take things to another level. I had a solid team around me, and I knew that if I continued to build and add to my team that, in the words of my Virgo partna Swizz Beatz, "the sky is not the limit, it's just the view."

In recognizing the direction of my fate, my intuition, my voice started telling me, *You need to get out of your record deal.* That was the only way for me to grow and truly become the artist God created me to be. I assumed it wouldn't be simple, and I had no idea what that would look like, but one morning I woke up and called Chris and told him I didn't want to be on the label anymore. The general response I got was, "You can't do that. You can't just get off a label like that."

I was pretty sure his team thought I was looking to go sign with Cash Money because of my strong relationship with Wayne. But that wasn't my motivation at all. I just needed freedom, and my voice was telling me that it was time to become more independent and step firmly into my purpose. While I was grateful for everything the people at the label had put into our group, I believed it was time for me to step into something greater.

I was told I'd need to pay $100,000 in order to get out of my record deal. Part of me believes they asked for that number because they didn't think I had it. Maybe they had other reasons for asking for that number. Either way, I had it. I didn't have much more than that, but I had a little over that in an orange Nike shoebox at the crib. If paying was my only option, it had to be what it had to be.

I paid the hundred grand to get out of the deal and agreed to give them a point on each of my next three albums. Now let me tell you, a point is essentially one percent of an artist's royalties. That may not sound like a lot, but it is. Let's say an album makes a million dollars, then that one point is ten thousand. This is in addition to the points distributed between the label, producers, and possibly anybody else who put a lot of work into the project. A lot of hit-making producers might get one to five points, and that's for producing a banger. To give away a whole point is definitely a sacrifice that would come out of my royalties.

We currently live in a culture where it's in vogue for people to say "Bet on yourself." It damn near has almost turned into a cliché. You'll hear that a lot in professional sports: "So-and-so bet on themselves and didn't sign the deal." Well, I've actually been there and done it. It's a gamble just like anything else, but if you are tapped into your inner self, you can mitigate the risk. In order to place the right bet on ourselves, we first need to know ourselves. In his book *Know Thyself*, author Na'im Akbar says, "The dimension of the self represents that layer of individual personal experiences that have occurred in one's lifetime. If we understand our souls as the universal core of life that is the essence of our being, entering into our particular life experience and life space, then the experiences of this lifetime represent our unique and special journey."

The tally of my life experiences has created an inner well for me to draw from when I'm calculating any risk. If I'm tuned into that well and my inner voice, I already know the gamble will work out for me, even when it might not seem that way immediately. In the end, I'll always be right where I'm supposed to be.

I went solo, started doing shows, and making a name for myself as a solo act. I legit did a show in every state in the country, from North Dakota to Florida. My reputation started gaining even more traction, and it didn't take long for people and labels to start reaching out. Every day a different label would contact my team, and every day I was sitting down with a different label representative. This was during a time when labels had recently started doing this thing called a 360 deal. A "360," what they call it in the industry, is an exclusive contract between a label and an artist. In a 360, a record label not only got a share of the artist's music sales, but also percentages of revenue from other ventures, like concerts, merchandise, television appearances, or publishing.

When I took these label meetings, I had already done my homework and knew exactly what I wanted to talk about. I had all the information ready. For me, I was really interested in seeing what they had and what they brought to the table globally. I was already a household name domestically as an independent artist. I gathered that from my blowing up inside the Chitlin' Market, which is where I made my first million. I did shows at nightclubs for twenty, thirty, sometimes forty, even fifty thousand a night. Once I started to move outside the Chitlin' Market without a deal, I obviously knew I could be amplified if I had some creatine backing me. A label with some global pull. I like to call labels "creatine" because they add a little bulk to whatever you already got going on. They can't make or break you, but they can add something to whatever movement you already got. And I already had it, I just needed the world to experience it.

I would go into these meetings and ask the labels what they had going on internationally and how they could help me reach a broader audience. I wanted specific details, not pitches. Labels will try and hit you with the cookie-cutter pitch every time. I had to let them know that I was a custom nigga, so I needed custom presentations. During each meeting, at some point the representatives would start yapping about a 360 and how we could parlay that money to help boost my career this way or that.

By that time, I wasn't really listening to much of what they had to say because I was piped up. I was turned up. I had leverage. I knew my value and wasn't trying to hear nothing about them having more access to my money or my brand. I had already done that dance. I had already left that dance with gold cups and T-shirts. My voice was guiding me toward something new. I'm not saying anything was wrong with how they approached their business, but I just wasn't interested. Everybody seemed to be offering five- or six-album 360 deals. I continued to pass.

I eventually found my way back to Def Jam. Imagine that. We would go on to have two meetings.

Honestly, I wasn't all the way present for the first one. It was more like a revenge meeting. I wanted to let them know I was still out here doing it big. I wanted to let them know I had stayed on top without them. But after that first meeting, *something told me* to get my ego out the way, and not let my ego block any potential blessings. I took a second meeting with them and was more engaged in that one.

I ended up signing a solo deal minus the 360, and minus the five- or six-album commitment. I signed a four-album deal. Today, that deal has been fulfilled. When I signed it, I had developed so much leverage that I could demand that type of thing. I'm not saying I was so business savvy that I worked the system. I'm saying I had developed the kind of knowledge and leverage where it was my way or the highway.

When I was taking those meetings, I was ready to walk at any point in time. I had paid Chris $100,000 and a point on three albums to get out of my first Def Jam deal. I had experienced the success of betting on myself. Ultimately, now I'm on my third passport. The international aspect helped me become more of a worldwide name. As a solo artist, my stage moniker would eventually become 2 Chainz. I done heard 2 Chainz in different languages in different countries around the world. And as it relates to that hundred grand I had to give up to be released from my DTP deal, and I mean this very humbly, I got that on me right now.

PART II

FOUNDATION FIRST

God is love and love never fails. Keep on loving unconditionally. Believe me, you don't go through any more than anyone else. Be strong and carry on. God is with you. I always understood where you are coming from, and believe me, there's nothing new under the sun. Also, the father and son are one. Can you dig it. We are all put on this earth to do our best. To love God, self, and fellow man, and our woman. The strong survive, the weak fall by the wayside. And we all have different paths and ways to go. Still God is in charge. The more you pay your trials and tribulations, the more God will bless you for being a faithful and good servant. You're alright, and everything and everybody is alright. Just keep on praying and believing, child.

—Pops (through a prison letter)

IX

B.O.A.T.S.
(Based on a T.R.U. Story)

On my first solo project I had the opportunity to work with some amazing artists. I worked with Ye (Kanye) on the creative side. Virgil (Abloh) designed my first cover, which was black and gold with two actual chains being the only image. In thinking about the visual representations for the album, I sat in meetings with phenomenal artists and witnessed the seriousness with which they treated artistic work. That was extremely inspirational. I mean, they had real think tanks where everybody would come with their own ideas and individual creativity. Those moments were not only vital to the artistic production of my first album but also a reminder of how important it is to keep brilliant people around me.

They say you're only as strong as your weakest link, and during the creation of my first album, artistically and musically, we had no weak links. Everybody had a voice; everybody had a role. Everybody was tuned and tapped into the highest realms of their individual creativity. Man, everybody was listening to their inner voices, which created crazy momentum for what would eventually become a masterpiece.

I remember moving around in 2012 before my album came out and going to the All-Star game in Orlando. Even though I had already known that I was one of them ones, I was shocked to see how many people there knew it too. As soon as I walked in, everybody was yelling "2 Chainz." Like everybody on the floor, from LeBron to Dwight Howard. That All-Star game was one of them ones with legendary ballers: Kobe, D Wade, D Rose, Carmelo Anthony, all kinds of killers in their prime. My seat for the game wasn't the best. I was up in the stands with the general population, probably like twenty rows up. My jewelry was shining though so I wasn't tripping. I had already been a fan of some of those players, like LeBron (who's a good friend of mine now) and D Rose, which made it wild to hear everybody yelling my name: "2 Chainz, 2 Chainz."

I'll never forget sitting in my seat and looking down toward the floor, knowing that's where I was supposed to be. You ever had that feeling? It could be at work or in some kind of social setting. Maybe you're waiting in line at the club and see folks walking past the line and right in. There are moments, whether literally or figuratively, where you just know you not where you supposed to be. When something is telling you that you either should or deserve to be someplace else. I'm fine being in the general population when I want to because I come from the margins. I come from the dirt. But I'm also a front-row kind of nigga when I want to be, and something wasn't sitting right with me when I looked down toward the floor and saw my peers enjoying the festivities.

I got to moving around, moving how I normally move. Remember the phrase "act like you're supposed to be there"? That's been me my entire life. I won't say I "acted" because I'm not an actor, but I've always moved like I knew what I was doing. Most of the time I do.

From the time I got my first pack to my first time in the studio, I've always presented with T.R.U. confidence. (More on T.R.U. later.) And because that's in me, I started making my way courtside like *fuck it*. I mean, I'm walking past security like *fuck it*. Mind you, they're asking for my badge as I'm moving, but I'm not making any eye contact, I'm just acting like I knew what I was doing. At some point, I remember seeing Wayne courtside. I knew once I got close enough for him to see me, I'd be all good. So, I just kept on walking.

The closer I got to courtside, the more celebrities I started to see. The person I remember the most was Mary J. Blige. She was damn near courtside, and she was like, "Hey 2 Chainz." I can't lie, it was one of the few times in my career that I was a little surprised somebody as iconic as Mary knew who the fuck I was. I was and still am such a fan of Mary J. Blige. I remember thinking, *Damn, you know me? You really know me?*

Immediately after that I ran into Drizzy Drake. He was sitting courtside chilling. Now, me and Drake had already met back in '08 on a tour with Wayne, so we already had a rapport. The vibes between us had already been established, so it was like seeing an old acquaintance. Before Drizzy even opened his mouth, I told him, "Boy, have I got something for you." He was like, "Cool, let's work." I kicked back the same sentiment, "Hell yeah, let's work."

Here's the funny thing about confidence. It can have you stuck between a rock and a hard place real fast. I told Drizzy I had something for him but was lying the whole time. I didn't have shit for him, not a damn thing. I was literally just capping. What I did have outside the arena was a tour bus that I'd paid for, and that tour bus had a studio in it.

In his book *The Luck Factor*, British psychologist Richard Wiseman wrote:

> People are often convinced that these opportunities are the result of pure chance. They just happen to open the newspapers at the right page, come across the right page on the Internet, walk down the street at the right time or go to a party and meet the right person—but my work revealed that these seemingly chance opportunities are the result of lucky people's psychological make-up. The way they think and behave makes them far more likely than others to create, notice and act upon chance opportunities in their lives.

I left that basketball game and went straight to the tour bus ready to work. Shit, I had an opportunity in front of me that I had to capitalize on. I told my engineer, a guy named Jack, to find something we could put the boy Drake on. He got right on it, and at the time it was a producer by the name of Mike Will whose production we had in the vault. Back then Mike Will would be so persistent that at times it would irk me. I couldn't be mad at his hustle though, and how much he wanted to make things happen. I'm talking about mixtape days.

I was thinking about my boy Mike Will, and I pulled up one of his beats. There was this little melodic part on the beat, and I was thinking, *I bet the boy Drake would kill this part*. I was so sure of how great our chemistry would be on the song that I did my verse right there on the bus. I did my verse like *boom* and sent it over to Drizzy. He responded immediately like, "Man this shit hard. Let me sit with it for a minute."

Weeks started to go by, and I hadn't heard from Drake. The anxiety of waiting was killing me because I was wondering what he was doing with the track. Another week went by, and my impatience had reached its height. *Something told me* to do another verse to liven up the track and send it over. I did another verse, which meant I was on both the first verse and the third verse. The track still had holes on the second verse and there was no hook. It took a little bit to hear back from Drake, and when he finally sent me something, I plugged that shit right in. Man, I Goddang knew it was a hit right away as soon as I heard, "Real niggas say TRU, you ain't never told no lie." Fucking epic.

"No Lie" would go platinum. It became one of the biggest songs from my debut solo album. Another record that went platinum was "Birthday Song," featuring Kanye West. I had performed at South by Southwest, and both Ye and Big Sean came out and rocked with me.

We ended up kicking it on my tour bus, and I remember sitting down with Ye and playing him some beats. There was one song I had been sitting on that I just knew was a Ye song. I knew he would love the song. Ironically, when I played it for him, he was like, "Man, play something else." I was surprised and disappointed. I went on and started playing some trap shit, some ratchet shit, a bunch of other shit I had in the vault.

Something told me to go ahead and play shit that I could never imagine Ye on. I played "Birthday Song" with just me on it and watched him completely come alive. Up until that point he seemed completely bored with the shit I was playing.

"Nah, that's the one," he said out loud. He was completely sure. Ye jumped on the song, and afterward I got it mixed and mastered. I sat on the song for a minute because I didn't want to do anything with it before letting him hear the final version. Ye so busy that I didn't want to bother him, but eventually we ended up being in the same place doing some kind of fashion show together. I was in the back picking out looks, and I remember saying to Ye, "I need you to check this out."

I played the finalized version of "Birthday Song" for him, and homeboy was like, "Man, gimmie that." He took it, sat with it, and put a new mix on it. It came out crazy. That's part of Ye's genius. His creativity is so expansive, and his ear for music is just really profound. We knew we had a hit. We moved quick to find a director to shoot a video for it. We had a blast on that set. The track was dope, the video was fire. That whole motherfucker was out of here.

It's been said that people are sponges, and we learn most of our valuable information from the time we're born until around first or second grade. Those experiences become the data that makes up our personalities.

By the time I was in the second grade, I knew how to do everything from ride a bike to tying my shoes to many other things. I also experienceed domestic violence and a drug raid by the second grade. With intuition, with inner feeling, I have been able to trust myself. I had to learn how to be okay with something seeming weird, or feeling weird or out of place, or when things seem unexplainable. Being connected with your inner self is truly an unexplainable act. One that is connected to the higher power. It can feel like you have superpowers.

Sometimes you may even feel like you're psychic and see something before it happens. I swear, I can think of someone, and then that person will call me or text me. Or I might call or text someone because their energy might come to me out of the blue and they'll be like, "I was just thinking about you." And I'll be like, "I know." That's how strong my mind is, my telepathy is.

When you have that voice you hear, you got to be open-minded and willing to trust yourself, knowing that voice is coming from a safe place. It's coming from a true place. Although, trauma ridden, or struggle ridden, or even if you're born with a silver spoon in your mouth, it's very important to grow and learn, learn and grow. You shouldn't be afraid to be odd. You shouldn't be afraid to be different. Hence, my classic record "I'm Different" with the repetitive hook and dope lyrics.

As great as it was to have experienced the success of records like "Birthday Song" and "No Lie," "I'm Different" going platinum hit harder than any of my previous successes.

"No Lie" went platinum, but that had Drake on it. "Birthday Song" went platinum, but that had Ye on it. "I'm Different" was the first time I went platinum for a song that was solely mine: it was fifty percent producer and fifty percent me. Totally my idea, and a million people bought it. A million people had bought my idea.

To be clear, I'm not saying there's anything wrong with collaboration. I enjoy working with other artists. When the chemistry is right, it's a great way to create high-level music. Me and other artists have collaborated to make monster hits, but I'm a person who prefers to drink out of the cup of reality. I wasn't doing too much celebrating or getting too intoxicated by the success of certain hits when other artists contributed greatly to the music and helped get the idea across to listeners.

With "I'm Different," it was just me. It was my song, and I was finally able to get inebriated off that truth, that cup of reality. I was in London about to go onstage when I got the news that the song had gone platinum. I remember looking in the mirror and patting myself on the back. I thought about all the labor I'd spent in the studio busting my ass every damn night. I smiled. Not just for me but for my people, too. A million people was rocking with us. A million people had bought my idea.

My intuition was a driving force behind the creation of "I'm Different." I had been different my entire life, and *something told me* to talk about what it means to be different and stand out.

The production was a West Coast beat by DJ Mustard. Mustard is from LA. I actually met Mustard, YG, and Ty Dolla $ign at my studio at 5540 Old National when I had still been trapping. My guy Poon brought them niggas through the studio around the time when YG and Dolla $ign had a hit song called "Toot It and Boot It." I already felt like me and Mustard had camaraderie, so it was easy to catch good vibes when we started working on "I'm Different."

The West Coast has never had a problem with being super liberated or standing out. They have never cared about what people think of them and have been standing on individualism since early on. I mean, think about N.W.A. West Coast folks would dress, look, and express themselves to match what they felt inside. I always thought that was dope.

Choosing a West Coast beat that had only maybe four or five sounds was the perfect pairing for the direction of that song. A different kind of beat for a different kind of song. "I'm Different" was a song meant to celebrate all individuals, everybody. Whether you're queer, straight, or whatever. I particularly thought about the outcasts out there, the unique individuals who, like we say now, stood on business to protect their energy and their aura. Experiences become data that ultimately informs your personality. I wanted to create a vibe that people could relate to, however you choose to be different and T.R.U. to yourself. "I'm Different" is your anthem.

X

REMIND THEM BY REBRANDING

Tity Boi is the name I grew up with. That's what everybody called me, Tity Boi. My family called me Tity Boi because I'm an only child and grew up spoiled. It's some real country shit.

Me and my mama have always been best friends. We've always been connected at the hip. The people who really knew me growing up started calling me "Tit," or "Tity Baby," or "Tity Boy." My pops used to call me "Tity Man." It was my family's way of saying, "Boy, you stay on your mama's tity," or "You always on your mama's hip." It was both endearing and making fun of our closeness. It's been with me my entire life. My close dogs or day ones call me Tit til this day.

In the early 2000s when I signed with Ludacris and Disturbing Tha Peace, I didn't have a rap name. I went by my childhood name, Tit or Tity. That was the first name I rapped under, and I rapped under that name for a while.

It all was cool until folks started looking at me crazy. I started to sense people taking the name the wrong way. When people would hear my rap name, especially women, I started sensing they assumed it had some sort of sexual connotation. Like I was just some kind of sexed-up, horny rapper walking around grabbing women. I wanted to tell people, "Naw, naw, this just some country shit. This just some bona fide neckbone and chitlin' Southern type shit." It didn't have nothing to do with being freaky.

Most of the rappers had more traditional rap names like MC this, or Lil that, Shorty this, or Big that. My name wasn't traditional. It was Southern, and it was country. It came from the cracks of the apartment buildings we had lived in. It was straight from my granny's and pops's mouths. It came from trapping in the streets and being my mom's only son. It didn't have nothing to do with being a freaky nigga but everything to do with being a real one.

Looking back, I can now laugh thinking of a set featuring a bunch of emcees with traditional rap names: "Tonight we have a special show for all you ladies and gentlemen. We have the emcees you've been waiting to hear. We'll get the show started with MC Fireman. He knows how to set the stage on fire. And then after that, we'll turn it up a notch with Lil Go Getter. If you heard his single 'I Go Get It,' then you know you're in for a treat. But that's not where the entertainment ends. We'll be taking it even further with Shorty Rock Da Mic. One of the coldest bar spitters in the game."

Then my name is mentioned: "And just when you think the ride can't get any doper, Tity Boi will be here to take us home." Yeah, I guess I can understand how that might've thrown some people off. Probably had people like, "What in the pornography is going on here?" But it is what it is. It was what it was. I can laugh at it now. My childhood name was Tity Boi. Everybody who's known me from jump knows that'll always be my name.

---

2 Chainz just kind of fell into my lap. Almost like a spiritual thing that just came to me. For the life of me I can't remember my verse, but at some point, I said something like "Tity, 2 Chainz."

From then on, the name just started to have a life of its own. It became a momentum, an energy that just kept on growing. Isn't that how a lot of great ideas manifest? They come almost like accidents. Sometimes you're just saying some shit, and before you know it, it becomes more significant than you intended, than you could have imagined.

They say God speaks through us all. When you're properly aligned, you hardly realize when that divine inspiration is flowing through you. Incredible things can just seem ordinary in the moment. I'm still surprised at how 2 Chainz has become some shit that has stuck and built itself out. The name has represented both my journey and my growth. I think of it as one chain representing who I currently am, and the other chain representing who I aspire to be.

For a long time, since the nineties, I've had one chain tatted on me, but God eventually gave me the movement attached to the name. He literally gave it to me. I can't tell you the day, the time, or exactly how it happened. All I know is it fell into my lap, and I'm grateful for it. I remember one day just deciding to go by the name and started telling people on the scene to call me 2 Chainz. I started telling the DJs to introduce me as 2 Chainz. The rest is really kind of, as they say, history. The people most close to me still call me Tit, and even some of my closest friends in the industry. Lil Wayne calls me Tit because we've been rocking since way back in the day.

I've recently started to become known as Toni. You'll hear me referring to myself as Toni in my more recent records. Toni is an expansion of 2 Chainz and a part of my branding.

Here's some game for you: If you're involved in any kind of business, then you should always think through a business lens. An important pillar of business is knowing how to effectively rebrand your business every three to five years. You might see it happen with your favorite club or restaurant. The name and makeup might change, but the ownership and overall vibe could be the same. People get tired of the same brand and branding. It can get stale. You should stay thinking of ways to keep your brand fresh. (More on game later.)

I am a walking business, a walking brand. The name Toni comes from our old studio, 5540 Old National, our whole trap, calling each other Toni. Toni was like another name for cocaine, think Tony Montana. We were all different variations of Toni: Black Toni, Big Toni, Little Toni. That name from way back has always kind of stuck, even to this day. Toni represents an aspect of my business and personal maturation. I'm grown and will forever walk in every sacred name God has given me: Tity Boi, Tity Man, Hair Weave Killer, Daniel Son, the Necklace Don, Bandtonio, 2 Chainz, and Toni from the motherfucking apartments.

XI

5540 OLD NATIONAL

Me and my dog Dolla had been doing this rap thing for a while. Around the mid-2000s, we started taking it seriously, and around that time we got the Def Jam/ Disturbing Tha Peace deal under our group name Playaz Circle.

While we were grateful to have the record deal, at that particular time, we had to ask somebody at the label for studio time. We couldn't just record whenever we wanted to. It could never be sporadic or spontaneous, we would need to preplan. This is very difficult for artists because sometimes you never know when that creative bug might bite, and you need to run to the studio to lay down an idea. That really affected our ability to work toward being great. If you want to be great at anything, you need to put in the work. You need to be able to work at whatever whenever you need to.

Malcolm Gladwell talked about the ten-thousand-hour rule in his book *Outliers*. He basically says that ten thousand hours of practice at something is the magic number before you can become great at it. The word *practice* is important because spectators might celebrate a great stage show or a great athletic performance but not consider how many hours of practice went into it. How you practice becomes a part of your work ethic.

Kobe Bryant is maybe my favorite basketball player ever. In fact, I got *24* on my knees after his passing to honor him. Rest in peace, Kobe. There are so many amazing Kobe stories about his work ethic and how he approached practice. Byron Scott, his former teammate and coach, said he found Kobe as an eighteen-year-old rookie shooting in the dark two hours before practice had even started.

One of my favorite stories is from Shaq, who said, in his book *Shaq Uncut*, Kobe used to practice without a ball: "You'd walk in there and he'd be cutting and grunting and motioning like he was dribbling and shooting—except there was no ball. I thought it was weird, but I'm pretty sure it helped him."

Motivational speaker Dr. Eric Thomas once said, "You can't control how long I practice," encouraging people to control what they can. Controlling what we could was me and Dolla's thinking when we decided to invest in our own studio.

At that time, we were still trapping, still in the streets. We found a location on Old National: 5540 Old National. Let me back up. It was actually Dolla's idea to get the studio. He was like, "We need a spot, we need our own spot." He actually found the spot, and when he did, he hit me like, "Tit, I got us a spot." It was behind this Jamaican restaurant, an African store, and a barbershop. It was right next to Skatetowne roller rink.

I remember going over there and checking the spot out. I think Dolla already had a discussion with the owners or whatever because we were able to just put our coins together and get the spot relatively quickly. It was a night in either late November or December when we closed on the spot. I remember it being real cold outside. The space was freezing. That same night we went to Walmart, got these little space heaters, and plugged them in trying to warm the spot up.

We sat inside there in the cold. We didn't have any furniture yet. We actually sat on pallets and bricks and just smoked. We were just smiling at each other on some *this is ours*–type shit. There was no TV. There wasn't even any electricity, which makes me wonder how we got those heaters to work. Propane. That's right. I remember now. We used propane tanks.

Over time we built 5540 out. We slowly worked on getting the space together. It soon became a place where all the hustlers came together to kick it, but it was a studio at the same time. It became one of those spots that the whole city pulled up on: gangsters, street niggas, chicks, hustlers, everybody. We was doing it. I pushed bags, and Dolla had his hustle going on. A couple of niggas sold drink and lean. Other niggas sold bricks, zips, and everything else. We were all eclectic with the hustling.

To get to 5540, you would turn off the main road and ride straight to the back. That's where we were at. We installed surveillance, so we could see people coming before they got there. We had a system on the door that allowed us to buzz you in from the surveillance TV. We'd look at the TV, see who it was, and then buzz you in if everything was cool. We had this big metal door. A kind of security door.

When you first came into 5540, you'd walk into an area that looked like a little office setup: it had a desk, a little computer, but really was just a place where people jugged. When you went through the first set of glass double doors there was a pool table. We had the pool table in the middle of the floor. All hustlers had a pool table in their spot. It was where everybody congregated. By the pool table. You'd shoot dice, shoot pool, put your cup of drink on the pool table, sit on the pool table and watch ESPN. It was actually a glorified piece of furniture. And we were so ghetto at the time that we painted the pool room red and green—like the Gucci colors—it was our Gucci room.

We did have a sofa in there too, but nobody really sat on it. If you kept straight ahead and exited the Gucci room, you'd find two other little rooms: a small room where I hung a bunch of my pops's old albums and a kitchen. The album room was like a little vibe room. There was also a barber chair in there so that everybody could keep fresh.

In the kitchen, we had a nice little setup. I remember we would have plenty of good food cooking in there. The boy Dolla loved to cook, so we'd have everything from seafood boils to soul food, just a little bit of everything to keep us fueled up. We also had niggas who would come over to drop or rerock some work right quick. Let's just say it was an all-purpose kitchen.

After you maneuvered past the kitchen, you'd make a right and there was the hallway. To the left was a bathroom not big enough for anybody to barely do anything. It was like an airplane bathroom—a very tiny lavatory. To the right there was a larger studio, and inside that studio was a very small makeshift studio. I had a lifting bench in there, a pull-up bar, and a dip bar. The same stuff I have in my studio today. Enough to keep me fit, keep my mind working, and keep me juiced up.

This was 5540, my first studio, where all the magic happened. Me and Dolla made some classic records there, but for years I remember kind of being one foot in and one foot out. Trapping today, rapping tomorrow.

After getting out of our deal with Def Jam and becoming a solo act, I went on the road with Lil Wayne. I want to say this was around 2007–08. When I was on tour with Lil Wayne, I had the opportunity to see how he actually moved. I saw what he did before a show, during, and after. I started to realize that regardless of how much money I assumed he had, this was how he moved every day. Like he was broke. Like it was a job. Like he needed to work to keep the lights on. Wayne would work all through the night. He had no set time for punching in or punching out. He also didn't approach his craft like a forty-hour workweek. He worked whenever he wasn't catching a nap.

After being on the road with Wayne, *something told me* I had to up my discipline. I remember thinking to myself, *Yeah, we got the studio. We got 5540. But I'm not rapping every day. I'm still trying to hustle. I'm still trying to do both. I got one foot in and one foot out. I need to be truer to the game, truer to rap*. There's a saying in most hoods: "If you're true to the game, the game will be true to you." I needed to start putting in more hours.

When I left the tour with Wayne and came back to the trap, I had quit selling bags cold turkey. Niggas was asking me for bags because I'd always had them. I had to keep telling them, "Shit, bruh, you know, I don't do that no more." And they were tripping like, "Man, come on with the bullshit. Let me get one of them bags." I just kept telling them the same thing: "I don't do that no more." People thought I was flexing. They thought I was capping, lying. "Man, come on. You can't just quit trapping cold turkey." I had to tell them I was serious. There was no way I could reach my level of superstardom I wanted to and still trap.

Something told me, "Put the bags down." A voice told me, *It's time to focus on this. I got something better for you.* Now, I should mention, when I retired from the trap game I had over half a million dollars. You dig what I'm saying. I was a trapper who really made my way and had it my way. And you know, I believe anybody selling weed should eventually be a millionaire. A lot of people trap, but I just believe that if you're a real hustler, then you should get some millions off it. The trap game had been good to me. There wasn't a need to keep going. I had been blessed up to that point.

I remember considering asking my pops to help me bury the money, but *something told me* at the time not to mention it to him. My pops was a hell of a nigga, and I sure do miss him. More than figuring out where to stash the money, I realized I had a bigger problem. The company I was keeping. I was still hanging around people who trapped. They were my friends, my guys, I went to high school with some of them and the whole nine. The cliché of how the company you keep can ultimately determine how successful you are at something is true, man. In high school, when I wanted to elevate my trap game, I surrounded myself with hardcore trappers. That worked for me back then. But once I wanted to elevate my rap career,

I knew I had to surround myself with more determined artists and musicians. I had to surround myself with people who were serious about their craft, people who worked on music and visuals like their lives depended on it.

There were also some events that happened that made me start to think that maybe I needed to separate myself and find a different studio, one that was solely my own. Even though I didn't want to do it.

I had always been someone who's up at all times of the night, but when I came back from the tour, I made it a point to go to the studio at night, to work at night. I wouldn't normally go in the daytime. I'd just sit in the house all day. But as soon as it got dark, I'd pop out and leave the house around 10:17 p.m. I remember that time because it was Gucci Mane's record company's name. Shout-out to Gucci, who was and still is like a cousin to me.

I would go to work at 10:17 every night, and most of the time, the guys that trapped would be gone by then. They almost had a cutoff period, almost like they were clocking out. I was beginning to move out of the "clocking out" mentality. Plus, with me cleaning myself up, there wasn't a time that I needed to get back outside and get to trapping. I'd stopped trapping, so I wasn't missing any money associated with it.

Everybody knew how I was beginning to work. The engineer working with me knew it. We'd get to working, pull up a beat, and that's when I'd get to being creative. That started happening and then all of a sudden, at me and Dolla's place, the light bill had got behind like three or four thousand dollars. I had heard about it through the grapevine. I heard the light bill was behind and that some of the guys thought that because I was on the road doing independent shows that I would pay for it. I remember thinking, *Y'all niggas selling bricks and bags, what y'all think I'm supposed to do. I ain't nobody daddy around here.*

That gave me the itch to look for my own studio. I felt like I had outgrown the situation. But I did stay down for a few more months. I remember Georgia Power came through, they came and took meter readings, threatening to turn our power off. The crazy thing was that we had a J working with us, J Black. J Black could get the lights turned back on no matter who turned them off. J Black would go get another fucking meter, and *boom,* the power would be back on.

At the same time, we were really doing illegal activities, and I was trying to break out and be this artist. I didn't need any negative attention, but I also didn't need anybody thinking I couldn't pay my light bill. I was thinking, *I'm popping and talking all this shit, and folks might be running around here saying I can't pay my light bill.* I don't need that.

The next thing you know, Georgia Power was willing to work something out with us because the light bill had reached eight thousand. They wanted four thousand immediately and four thousand on a payment plan. I said to myself, *You know what? I might have to get the fuck up out of here man.*

I ended up getting a new studio, my own, but continued running in the same circles. One of my people found me another studio spot, toward downtown. It was kind of like a loft, but I was able to make the best of it. Maybe the first week after I moved out of 5540 and let my guys keep it, it got shot up. I hadn't even had the new place for a week, didn't even have it set up yet. I'll never forget, soon after I got the new place, the Cleveland Cavaliers came to town shortly after Bron had returned to Cleveland. Me being the basketball fan I am and knowing that Bron and Kyrie would be in town, I had to pull up on the game. I'd been sitting courtside at the Hawks games forever anyways. I wasn't in my seat for thirty minutes before I got a call.

"Shawty, somebody just shot up the studio." I couldn't believe what I was hearing.

"What? Wait. What happened?"

"Fifty-five-forty. Somebody shot that motherfucker up." I was speechless.

Today, I still don't know what really transpired at the studio because I wasn't there. Somebody did lose their life that night, and the studio was infiltrated with bullet holes. Rest in peace. I'm not saying that my intuition or my voice told me to attend the game that night. It could've just been my being a basketball fan. But I was at the game when the incident occurred. It was probably around eight or nine o'clock.

I can't say I would've been at the studio when everything went down, but after the incident, my inner voice grew louder. Even though I had the new studio, something still didn't feel right about how I was moving.

In *The Luck Factor,* Wiseman says this about trusting our gut feelings when something doesn't feel right: "Deep down, they know that something is wrong, and often this rather odd feeling emerges as a kind of intuition—an inner voice or gut feeling telling them that they are kidding themselves. Some people listen to this inner voice and others choose to continue with their wishful thinking and self-denial."

I was gassing myself thinking I could change studio locations but not the particulars of how I was moving. People do this a lot. We might change cities and think that'll fix everything. Or we'll get a new job and think that's the fix. Then we get confused when those changes don't change our outcomes, or the outcomes of people close to us. I started to realize that the most important proximity change I needed to make was my own closeness to my intuition. I needed to be more tuned and tapped into my inner voice, my inner self.

After the incident, *something told me* it was time to completely go to another level; it was time to completely move on. That would keep my dedication and work ethic heading in the right direction. I didn't need to be across the street or around the corner from my intuition. I needed to be right inside that thing. That would be the only way for me to reach the full potential of what God had intended for me to become. And it's so unfortunate that one of the homies passed away. I still remember the good about 5540 Old National, the energy. A lot of hits were made there, a lot of heads were busted in there, a lot of people passed out in there. A lot of good gambling went on in there. A lot of good memories were made. A lot of the homies not with us anymore, a lot of them still are. But that's 5540 Old National. My first studio. It built resilience, it built toughness, it built some players.

XII

MISFORTUNES INTO FORTUNES

In the 2024 Run-D.M.C. documentary *Kings from Queens*, both D.M.C. and Reverend Run talked about the traumas that not only affected the group but each group member individually. No matter how folks might try and warn you about the demons that come with success in the public eye, nobody can really prepare you for the actual experience.

Shit, I know. Working with Wayne gave me a front-row seat to all the ways the industry can break you. The demands from your label, fans, friends, family, and your own creative desires can have you feeling like you're on that Freefall ride at Six Flags Over Georgia. I still don't know what me and my cousins loved about that ride. It'd take you all the way up, at least a hundred feet in the air, and then drop you all the way to the bottom.

I've always been conscious of how abruptly something that seems permanently upright can change on you.

I've seen plenty of artists enjoy that lavish ride to the top, and then, out of nowhere, the industry drops them back to the neighborhoods they came from. Like I mentioned in an earlier chapter, I call this "going down the ladder." But this drop is not like the ride at Six Flags. When the industry drops you, you don't get to the bottom and tell everybody how much fun you had. There's no happy adrenaline rush or high fives when you lose everything.

Industry stress is a real thing, and Run-D.M.C. experienced it all. In the documentary, D.M.C. went on about the pressures and stressors that came with being in such an iconic group. He talked about how it all led to his abuse of drugs and alcohol. He would have drinking binges between shows and on most days, he would just feel empty. All of this led to his not wanting to live anymore. What stood out the most to me was this one story he told about being in Yugoslavia with the group for an interview. The interview happened on the roof of the hotel they were staying at. After completing the interview, he noticed that the door leading to the roof hadn't been relocked. He saw that as an opportunity to end his life.

D.M.C. made sure Rev Run and Jam Master Jay went back to their rooms, and then bolted back up to the roof. He stood on the ledge. He was ready to jump. He was ready to end it all. But right before he was about to jump, he said he heard a voice: "You can't jump yet, D. You can't jump because they don't know who you are." That voice shook him out of his trance, and he got down from the ledge. He was seconds away from jumping before he heard the voice. Unfortunately, right after D.M.C.'s almost suicide, Jam Master Jay would be murdered at a studio in Jamaica, Queens. Rest in peace.

Not too long after Jam Master Jay passed away, D.M.C. got his life in order.

For me, watching the documentary and hearing D.M.C. discuss his desperation standing on that ledge, I couldn't help but notice how he looked up to the sky when he mentioned hearing a voice. The chills still run through me when I think about it. He stood on the ledge and was prepared to jump until he heard a voice.

I know that voice all too well. I also know why he looked up when he mentioned the voice. He probably didn't even notice that he looked up. It seemed like a reaction; it was a quick head raise that most people watching probably missed. Go back and watch the *Kings from Queens,* and when you get to that part, pay close attention. You'll see what I'm talking about.

That voice he mentions is what I've been talking about throughout these chapters. It's a spiritual voice, a divine one. He said the voice told him he couldn't jump because people didn't fully understand who he was yet. It also told him that the kind of ending he thought he wanted was not the one written for him. The voice that spoke to D.M.C. while he stood on that ledge is the same voice inside us all. We just need to listen when it shows up. Quiet your mind and it'll come when you need it.

Don't be afraid of it. Don't run from it. Lean into it. Just like D.M.C., you'll feel its reverence when it comes to you. You'll feel assured. It's coming from a higher source. It's coming from a loving source. The voice in your head is God.

If God is with me through everything, I can do anything. This belief started with letters, prison letters. Well, the foundation started before the letters, but I really began to understand how a higher power can cloak a person through my pops's letters. He used to write "God is love" at the end of all his letters. I started receiving the letters when I was a teenager, during one of the times my pops had got locked up.

Even though I was young, the statement touched something in me. "God" and "love" being mentioned in the same breath made sense; but back then I couldn't take the words any further. That's how it is when you're young. Things may leave an impression on you, but a lot of times we don't have the tools to take it much deeper. I was too busy trapping and hooping to think too deeply about "God" and "love." I've been a deep thinker my whole life, but with that statement, I didn't take the time to really consider what he meant. Over time as I've grown in this life, I've been able to piece together more and more what Pops was trying to tell me in those "God is love" letter closings.

God and love are the same. If love is involved in anything, then God is involved. I mean, think about nature and how rolling hills, sunsets, or oceans might pull our eyes right from our faces. Trees are the natural air-conditioning of our planet. They have other obvious benefits, too. We tend to think about natural phenomena as God's creations. If this is fact, then according to Pops, love must be involved in the making of it. We often forget that we are God's creations, too. This means love is a part of us. No matter how good or bad a situation might seem, love is always at our feet, if we step into it. Our jobs are to remember.

Once I started thinking like this and moving like this, I started to understand that my intuition, or the voice I hear, is from God. This means it comes from love. It must because it's served me every time I listened. I mean every time. It's as natural as them rolling hills.

This understanding has taught me that even though something may seem like a loss on the surface or on paper, I need to find optimism in it because I'm still here, which means God still wants me here, which means everything is all love. Bet. That's what Pops was reminding me of when he signed them letters "God is love." He wanted to make sure I remembered to maintain my faith, no matter what was happening on the outside. Trust my intuition. Trust my voice. All the things God equipped me with. It's all from God.

And like D.M.C., when the voice comes, be ready to look up, listen, and take proper action. Thankfully I've never been suicidal, but I know what the ledge of despair looks like, and I know what it is to have a voice guiding me on how to *get down from the ledge.*

In 2017, I was getting ready to headline my own tour. The tour was to start on a Wednesday. I was wired to get on the road and do one of the things I love to do: rock the motherfucking stage. I love to get in front of people who have invested time, money, love, and support. I never take for granted what a person at my show might go through to make it there. Some folks might need to make work arrangements. Some folks may have to find a babysitter.

Some folks might be spending money they don't have. All this to come rock with me. It's one of the best feelings. To be onstage and look into a crowd that knows all the lyrics to your songs. It's a synergy thing.

There's a back-and-forth soul exchange between the audience and me. I send the crowd energy, they send it back to me, and we start our contract that way. A back-and-forth agreement. Just like the call-and-response of the blues. This all started with field songs sung by slaves. The singer sings a line that cues an audience or other singers to respond. The technique goes way back, and it's something I incorporate in my shows.

If you've ever seen me perform, you know how I get down. The stage is a canvas, and I'm the painter. I've never been a performer to just stand or sit in one spot during the show. No disrespect to any performer who chooses to do that. But that's not me. I like to color the whole stage. My show has to be electric and eclectic. The audience has to feel the energy. In summer 2017, my album *Pretty Girls Like Trap Music* had dropped. That album had a bunch of classics on it. Records like "4 AM," "Realize," "Big Amount," and "It's a Vibe." That summer, I was preparing to tour for the album. Everything had been set up for an unforgettable ride.

The Sunday before my tour was to start, I decided to throw a big party as a way to celebrate before I got on the road. It was also a celebration of my mom and daughter, who have birthdays on the same day, July 26.

Back then, we'd have a party at my house for the kids, and then my mom would have her own pool party at her house at night. The party was going well, and there were a bunch of kids over. I have over a hundred acres at home, so there was plenty of space for folks to be themselves. It was the perfect Atlanta summer day. The breeze was right, the drinks were cold, and the music was banging. We had plenty of food and a bunch of parents there with their kids. I really tried to make it something where everyone could enjoy themselves. A bunch of my good friends and family came through.

We also had ATVs for the folks who wanted to ride. Me personally, I can chase adrenaline sometimes. People were riding ATVs or getting driven around on Can-Ams. There might've been a few Polaris. You know, everybody was just having fun.

I remember my neighbor at the time had around five kids, and they were cool. Some of them played tennis, some played volleyball, and some of them were ATV addicts like me. At some point, one of the neighbor's kids got on a four-wheeler and kind of started riding, you know, doing his thing. Because I felt like I was seasoned on them things, I decided to show him a thing or two. The funny thing is, you can be as seasoned as you want, but with an ATV you're always an accident away. My thinking was to go ride with him and kind of show all the kids a good time. I planned on doing some burnouts, some donuts, and really mess around. I remember getting on my ATV with some Adidas slides. The slides I wore had a Velcro strap. Very comfortable sandals. I can't stand those slides today. Here's why:

When I first got on to ride, I put the ATV in reverse, and when I did that, I cut that thing to the right. But, when I cut it to the right, something happened with the strap on one of the slides and my foot came right out. It's hard to explain because everything happened so fast, but my bare foot started dragging on the ground almost like some kickstand shit. Some kind of way. When I tried to steady the ATV, mind you I'm still going in reverse, I fell off.

The problem was that when I fell off, I put weight on that leg that didn't have a slide on, and it buckled. I felt my leg buckle and shift backward in a way legs shouldn't. I laid there for a second knowing something wasn't right. But I'm a player, so I was giving the impression that everything was cool. A couple of the kids saw it, and I definitely didn't want them freaking out. I told the kids to go and get my cousin Cat because he's big and shit. It didn't take long for Cat to run up and I told him, "Hey man, I might've fucked something up. Damn."

I was laid up in this field, and everybody was asking if I wanted them to call an ambulance. I didn't want all the circus that came with an ambulance, so I just asked them to help me up.

My people ended up driving a van through the field to get me. From there we went straight to the hospital. I got all kinds of MRIs and X-rays: elbow dislocated, knee broken. They put me to sleep to snap my elbow back in place. I remember my mom being the only family in the room with me.

I remember waking up from sedation and coming to. I remember the nurses asking, "Do you know who you are? Do you know where you are?" I was really groggy but definitely understood what they were asking. I said, "Yes, I know who I am." They said, "Who are you?" And I said, with a serious face, "I'm Michael Jackson." Boy, my mama said, "Aw shit. I'm getting the fuck up out of here. I don't got time to be playing with this boy. I'm going to my party." Ha. My mama has always been good for a timely joke.

I ended up staying for a couple of days. The funny thing is that I stayed because the hospital couldn't find a wheelchair big enough for me. I had to order a special kind of wheelchair. I can't say I didn't enjoy my stay though.

I floated those days I spent in the hospital. I would take what I called these morphine dreams. The floating process was so easy and efficient. Whenever you're in pain, you just hit this little morphine button, and *boom,* you knockout immediately. It didn't take long for my management to start asking about the tour. They wanted to know if we should just cancel it because I was in bad shape. I didn't want them to even announce what had happened or for anybody to know what was going on. Tickets had already been sold, and the first night was in Arizona in just a few days. I told them I needed some time to think.

Two days later, they needed a decision. "Bro, we got to decide. We got a tour coming in a couple of days." *Something told me* not to worry, that everything would work out. That same *something told me,* "This is an opportunity for you to be creative, to be an artist." I just didn't know what I was going to do.

There's always a silver lining to everything. I don't view accidents as accidents. What's for me is for me. If you change one thing, then you change everything, right? It's like that butterfly-effect thing I mentioned. I knew laying in that hospital bed that the accident had to happen, but I also knew I had a tour to do. My knee was broken, but my spirit was together.

I thought about it for a minute, and then it hit me. I told them, "Man, we got the album called *Pretty Girls Like Trap Music,* right? It's all pink. What if we had a pink wheelchair or something. What if we acted like I'm supposed to be in a wheelchair, make it all intentional? Let's make it a production, almost like a play." I'll never forget how big their eyes got when I said that. It was like the most obvious thing that none of us had thought of until then.

Nobody asked any questions. Management had heard me loud and clear and got to work. We found a guy that did custom wheelchairs. He made a pink one and flossed it out with rims. We found dancers and added that piece to the show. One of the dancers dressed up in a nurse's outfit. She stayed close to me during the show like she my personal nurse. She was a great dancer too. I mean, she was a professionally trained dancer. That added an entirely new dimension to the show.

We really ended up taking the stage-show idea to another level. Everything was coming together. At no point did I consider canceling the show. I couldn't let my fans down. The tour had shows in New Orleans, Dallas, Oakland, Portland, St. Louis, Detroit, Philadelphia, Miami, and Las Vegas, to name a few. There was a total of thirty-five dates. I wasn't going to let my fans down.

The first show in Arizona, no one had known about my accident. That night I didn't know what to expect. I flew out there via private jet because I didn't want anybody to see me on crutches. Learning how to move from crutches to wheelchair and wheelchair to crutches was very humbling. It's the small day-to-day things in life that we take for granted.

When the show started, I rolled out onstage in my wheelchair and the crowd went fucking crazy. I wasn't sure if they were buying the wheelchair being a part of the show or not. It didn't matter. The energy was up. The love had felt so real that I made an announcement in the middle of the show. "Yo, I broke my leg, but nothing could stop me from being here with you guys."

They went fucking crazy again. That energy turned me up. "*Something told me* to come out here and do this for y'all tonight. *Something told me* to fight through adversity. *Something told me* I could still have my way without being able to walk."

You know, not being able to walk for a few months will humble you. You even watch the amount of water that you drink because you don't want to keep getting up to use the bathroom. I wasn't even drinking that much water because I got tired of all that. But it made me a better person, a stronger person, a more resilient person and a more respected person. I was able to fight through adversity.

And another thing was that the guy who made the wheelchair for me died before the tour was over. Even today I consider him one of my angels because who else would come into my life like that, at a time like that, when I really needed an angel, when I really needed him, then disappear from my life, like that, if he wasn't an angel?

Coming from the Southside of Atlanta and the conditions I came from, I understand positive thinking may not immediately change our environment. I get that, and I'm sensitive to that. It doesn't mean you wake up and everything is peaches and cream. But it can be the difference, like I experienced at a young age.

I watched my parents go to prison, and still told myself, "I'm getting straight As in school and buying my mama a house when I get older." And I did that shit. I'm not telling anybody to praise any messenger if it ain't God, but it's alright to pay attention to the messages that speak to you.

The message "God is love" and my positive thinking eventually led to me being on that stage in Arizona, broken leg and all, pink wheelchair and all, to start the Pretty Girls Like Trap Music tour. My vision created a set with the same tore-down pink trap house that appeared on the album cover. The word *T.R.A.P.* was sprayed across the second-story windows. We dressed it up with lanterns that had the whole motherfucking stage glowing. When I was spitting my verses, it almost felt like an out-of-body experience.

I can honestly say that my whole life I've been an optimist. I became even more optimistic once I started understanding my pops's phrase "God is love." Had I fallen into a space of self-pity or self-doubt, that tour would've never happened. I had every excuse to cancel, and based off the reality of my condition, people would've understood. But when something happens to me, I try to look at the other door, sometimes the back door, to find some kind of optimism. I have experienced obstacles, setbacks, inconveniences, and disappointments like we all have. When these things occur, my initial impulse wants to say, "Why shit be happening to me all the time?" But I catch myself quick, and that's usually followed by a strong intuition of how I can make the situation work in my favor, how I can turn a misfortune into a fortune.

XIII

GOD IS LOVE

Rest in peace to pop, he was an OG
"Good Drank"

When I speak about intuition, I think about the importance of the senses. I recently went to Hawaii with my family, and a visually impaired cashier was working at the airport. I thought about how intuitive he had to be, out there on his own, making it. To be in survival mode on his own, ringing up what we got, figuring out the money, doing the calculations.

My daughter peeped that he had an impairment a little later, but I peeped it early on. The senses. If you think about the senses, you think about people who may even be hearing impaired but still communicate through sign language, or articulate how they feel through body language, it's really incredible.

When I think about the senses and how intuition ties into them, I think about my earliest memories of my pops. I think about the albums he kept in the house when I was growing up. I remember the Rick James album cover, *Street Songs*. He has the guitar with the tall red boots. I remember my pops would blast "Give It to Me Baby" and "Super Freak." I definitely remember the New Edition *Candy Girl* album cover. The group was young then, and it seemed like every member was wearing leather. Man, I remember the song "Candy Girl," and "Is This the End." Had a young 2 Chainz looking for love way too young.

I remember Michael Jackson's *Thriller* album cover. He is reclining in that white suit. I remember Prince's *Purple Rain* cover and Al Green's *Let's Stay Together* cover.

My pops had all those records, and all those records created the soundtrack in my household growing up. Even today, the music on these albums awakens my senses and puts me right back in my childhood homes. In fact, I remember Al Green had turned into a preacher and my pops took me to see him preach. One time, we drove to Memphis to go sightseeing, and my pops took me to the Lorraine Motel. While we were there, he took me to Graceland. He would also sometimes take me on the road with him when he made dope runs. He'd bring jugs to pee in so we didn't have to stop for bathroom runs. I have memories of him peeing in a jug while my mom kept the steering wheel under control.

My pops was the biggest man I knew, the biggest man I'd ever met, and he probably was only like five nine. And when I say the biggest man, I'm referring to his aura, his spirit, his energy. I'm referring to what he believed in, his messaging. His teachings were those of a man with huge qualities. Although we didn't share a lot of one-on-one time, his teachings through jail calls, through letters, or whenever we were together have left life impressions on me. The last seven years of his life, he stayed with me. I was able to gain more respect for not just him but the way

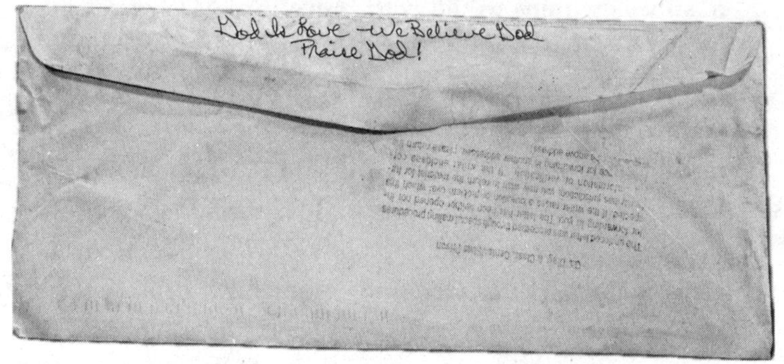

Thanksgiving 2003: letter from Pops.

the world works. I was able to better understand that in life there are ups and downs. When people say life be lifeing, it's just like you're not going to have a winning streak forever. I had to learn to be able to accept that. I was not always going to be on top. Life is a cycle. It's important to maintain perspective at all times.

I break that idea down into three things: there's the positive space, then you have the gray area, and then you have like this negative space. I know that life is this three-hundred-and-sixty-degree circle that goes around and comes around. Sometimes when you're in a good place, you might shift into a gray area where it ain't so good. And maybe you'll try to get back into the good space, but something bad is inevitable. It's going to happen, it's a part of life. Just knowing that after the bad something good will happen is my own concept and theory that has served me.

My father came from an era in which he believed a woman couldn't raise a man. I've come to know that women are superheroes and would like to give a shout-out to my mom who did a damn good job raising me. My pops did a damn good job of making sure I was prepared for the real world.

To say *legendary* is an understatement. Real legend. Loved in the streets. Loved in the church. Loved in hustlers' DNA. His teachings have actually become some of the voices in my head too. Sometimes, I can actually hear his actual vocal tone in my head. Some of his teachings on being a provider, a protector, and being a man. Not letting certain people do certain things or violate me in certain ways. It has stuck with me forever.

I remember him potty training me at like two years old. One day he told me, just out the blue, "Don't let nobody touch your butt, son." It sounds funny to me now, but these are teachings from literally two years old that I remember. I remember the bathroom, the yellow wallpaper. I remember how small the bathroom was. The conversations I've taken with me have become a part of my mental library and guided me throughout my life.

Me and my pops were always cool even though we didn't always stay together. We stayed together maybe the first seven years of my life and maybe the last seven years of his life. I've always been a man's man, which I learned from my pops. I admired his toughness and grit. He was also a God-fearing man. When he called from jail, he would always ask about the household. He would instill in me the importance of being a man, being the man of the house. This was a role I took on when he went to prison.

Since I was young, I took on the role of being the man of the house. It was always really just me and my mom, and I knew that it was my responsibility to make sure we were always okay. It was my responsibility to make sure nothing ever happened to her. I'm talking about even when I was eight, nine, or ten. I knew that our safety and security were on me. This was a role I gladly embraced. But embracing that role, I matured much faster than I should've.

My maturing fast was one of the reasons I started hustling so early. My pops had given me the game and the grace, and my mom didn't mind me hustling. My pops's lessons continued when I would go and visit him in prison. We would meet at this thick glass window. He would pick up his phone, I would pick up the other phone, and we would talk. Other times, he and my mom would talk, and I would listen. Whenever I was about to leave, he'd put his hand on the glass, and I'd put my hand on the glass. He would tell me that I was growing and how he could tell based off the size of my hands.

"Epps, your hands a bit bigger than they was the last time you were here." I remember all the sights, sounds, and smells of the prison. There were other families in the room, women with their children. There was no privacy. I remember the other prisoners on the other side. Some of them had pain on their faces. Some of them had joy on their faces. Some of them talked like they were saying something about regret. Others talked like they were saying something about plans once they got out. I couldn't hear what they were saying, but I believed I could feel them. They looked just like the men I knew from my life experience. I knew their struggles and their codes. I knew what made them tick. Each time the white deputies walked us out, I remember seeing the nightsticks, hearing the keys jingling, smelling the desperation.

On one occasion, I went to my grandfather's house because my pops stayed with him. This was before my grandfather passed away. I remember my grandfather saying, "Hey man, your dad went to court today, and they locked him up." At this point, my pops was probably in his late sixties or early seventies. He was definitely too old to still be dealing with the system.

I was like, "What in the world is he doing going to jail?" I was like, "He always in jail," and my granddaddy started saying some of the meanest things about him. He would talk to me very dearly but always said really mean things about my pops. He would tell me how he wasn't shit, and did this, and fucked with this, and caused all this. I would always listen with respect because that was my granddaddy, but it never swayed what I thought of my father. I knew who he was and loved him for it. I knew what he was and loved him for it.

One year, one month, one week, I found out he was about to be released from prison. Around the mid-2000s. I knew I wanted to be there for him even more than ever. He was getting up there in age, and I wanted us to spend more time together. I had a house, and I had a hustle that supported the people who depended on me. At the time it was just me, my wife Kesha, and my mom at the house. This was before I bought my mom her own house.

Something told me to go pick him up from Jackson County State Prison on the day of his release and bring him home with me. Forget all the nickel-and-diming and hustling he was doing. He needed some stability. He needed his son. We rode to go pick him up, and everything immediately after seemed like a whirlwind. My pops had plans. Lots of them. The first thing he needed to do was visit the bank. He had like nine thousand dollars stashed away. He wanted to get a cell phone and a new suit. We went to Verizon to get him a phone. One of the funny things was that they were asking him to come up with an email, and it didn't register to him that he could come up with an easy email but just make his password difficult to guess. This man's email was about twenty characters long. It had exclamations, dollar signs, and @ signs in it. I told him, "No, you don't have to do that." It was hilarious.

When we left Verizon, we went to the mall so that he could get fitted for a suit. It was there at some Men's Wearhouse that I told him, "I think you should stay with me for a while. I got you. I'm on my rap type of thing. I'm making some money. It'd be a good opportunity for us to connect." Now, he knew that I was rapping, but he didn't know the depths of it, or where I was going with it.

Thankfully, it didn't take much convincing and he agreed to stay with me. We moved him in and the two of us rekindled our relationship as father and son, as best friends. We became inseparable right away. We would ride together; we would hang out. He would come to the studio and hang out with me and my crew. He would smoke with us. He even started getting his little packs and moving some work on the low. He thought I didn't know, but I always knew what was going on. My pops would stay with me for about seven years.

Let me rewind. My pops had been in the army. He had this old-man physique where you could tell he had been fit before. He would still do his push-ups and dips. He would always walk around the house with his shirt off, like always. I used to be like, "Bro, put your shirt on." At one point, he had been gone for over a week, just gone. He called me and told me, "I'm in Alabama, I'm good, I'm fine. I'm down here in the hospital." I was like,

"What's going on?" He didn't tell me then, and he would never tell me.

One afternoon he was upstairs lying across his bed with the fan on. It was hot that day. I peeked into his room and saw this long slit under his chest, near his heart. I said, "Bro, what is that?" He said, "I had a little procedure done." I'm like, "What kind of procedure?" "Something with my heart. I'm fine, I'm cool though, I'm good." Around this time, I was in the middle of getting a record deal. I was doing a lot of shows, and from an independent standpoint, I'd made a reputation of being a very anticipated artist. Everything was coming together, and I wanted a new house, a nicer house.

My pops was the one who went with me to look at houses. He was my voice of reason. I remember looking at this one house. It was in Rick Ross's neighborhood, like in Fayetteville. We drove into this gated community, and the homes were nice and big, but they were also expensive. I had just enough money to get the house. It was like $700,000 or $800,000. I probably had about seven hundred. Me and Pops went to look at the doggone house, and I'll never forget my pops saying, "This a nice house, but can you afford it?" I knew I had enough money to afford the house, so the question was a no-brainer.

"Yeah, I can afford it."

"You got this kind of money?"

"Yeah, I got 'bout this much."

"You sure?"

"Yeah, I'm sure."

"Okay, cool. So how you gone furnish it?" I hadn't thought about that until he asked. I was only locked in on the cost of the house and nothing else.

"Oh shit. Damn Pop, you right. I didn't think about it like that." So, we left.

We kept on looking, and as time went on, we found this particular property that we had prayed for. With this one, everything went smooth, and we ended up getting it. There were some upgrades and painting we wanted done, so my pops would go over to check on the workers and the progress with everything. He would be like, "I'm just gonna go over there and check on these guys and make sure they doing right. You don't know what they might be doing at the house." I later found out that he started becoming friends with the guys. I saw pictures after he passed.

One cold November night, my pops ended up getting pneumonia from sitting in our vacant home while the guys worked. Since we hadn't been living in the house yet, there was no heat. He got pneumonia but overcame it. Then, another cold night shortly after, my wife called me while I was away and told me, "I just seen your dad come in the yard and get a big chain off the dog." I was confused because that didn't really make sense. I called him to see what was going on, and he told me. "Man, I missed the driveway and backed up into a ditch. I'm trying to get my truck out." I ended up calling my good friend Duck and told him to go over to my house and help get my pops out of the ditch. Duck was able to get my pops out of the ditch, but through the melee of everything, my pops caught pneumonia again.

He would get better again, and I ended up going on this trip out of town. Ironically, while out of town, I ran into this young lady who used to mess with one of my homeboys in Atlanta, and she was a doctor. Somehow, we started having a conversation about the heart.

I told her about all the health situations my pops had

been going through and explained this red heart-shaped pillow my pops had gotten from one of his hospital stays. The pillow had a bunch of signatures and messages on it: "Don't you come back." "You were great." "Stay good Mr. Epps." All these heartfelt messages were written on the pillow from the nurses.

The young lady listened to me tell the whole story, and then proceeded to tell me, "Your dad is going to die soon." I was shocked at how easily and casually she said it. I didn't sense any empathy or care in what she said. I immediately got offended and started calling her all kinds of inappropriate names. "Bitch, what are you talking about? What kind of shit is that to say to somebody?"

I didn't know it then, but I learned later that the pillow he received with those warm messages on it was one given to patients who had received care for some kind of heart congestion or heart failure. While I regret calling that young lady out of her name, I can't imagine a perfect way of responding to someone who told me that my father and best friend would be dying soon. I had just gotten him back in my life, and at that time that was one of the worst things anybody could've said to me.

In 2012, my pops had been getting sick again. He had been sick for a while, but it started to get worse. He was in the hospital not doing too good, and I stopped in to visit him. I remember it so clearly. We were just communicating, talking, having a good time, doing what Epps men do, what fathers and sons should do. I didn't want to take anything for granted, I wanted to make sure I spent as much time with him as I could.

I stayed with him for like two weeks, just in the hospital talking and joking. My pops was very sarcastic like most of the Epps family. We have a similar sense of humor, so when you get us two together, you could mistake it for improv or something. Laughing is something we cherished. One crazy fact about me is that I don't cry. I know that's hard to believe, but I can't remember the last time I cried. I'm not saying men shouldn't cry nor promoting that cliché. I'm speaking to how I was raised. My pops was an army vet who spent many years in prison. Being raised by him made me the ultimate man's man, even to a fault sometimes. I have the masculine spirit and stoic nature of that era. The era of hopping off the porch and going out and making money. There's nothing to cry about when you know that God is ultimately in control of everything.

My pops was a beast even when he was on something. A father's role in a boy's life is vital. Especially the Black boys where I'm from. These boys be needing someone to mirror themselves after. I know I needed it. Had I grown up without it, I would've still been tough based off how my mother had supported me and showed me how to survive, but having a man to connect with made a difference. It also created a DNA lineage for me to connect with. Do you understand how powerful it is to know where you come from? Knowing where you come from shapes your confidence.

My pops's stories preceded me. Me hearing trap superhero stories about a man whose DNA is inside me automatically piped me up throughout my life. He instilled a bunch of indirect game and knowledge in me. It wasn't like he sat me down in front of a chalkboard and pretended to be a teacher. I learned on the job. My pops didn't do everything right. He didn't do everything great. But I was able to build off the things I learned from him. I was able to customize the things that worked for me and make it my own fabric.

"What you got going on today?" my pops asked me after I was in the hospital with him for two weeks. I remember it was a Saturday morning, and he could sense something was off on my end. I was asked to do a show in South Georgia, and I didn't know how to tell him I needed to leave. I also didn't know how to tell him I didn't want to leave. I was in a real dilemma.

"I got a show, Pop."

"Oh yeah. Where about?"

"Somewhere in South Georgia. Savannah."

I had a tour bus at the time, but when it was time to leave for the show, I sent the homies to the venue on the bus without me. I wasn't sure if I was going to make it. I didn't want to leave. I told the homies I might come later on, and that I'd just drive myself. "Y'all go ahead, I'm going to chill with my pops for the moment. I'll drive down if I make it." And that was that. They were cool with it.

Me and my pops sat around eating sandwiches and fruit, laughing and reminiscing.

"Epps, you remember you started riding your bike before the second grade?"

"Yeah, Pop, I do. By the second grade I could do a lot of things on my own."

"Man, me and your mom was like, the hell he learn how to do that." Pops laughed while I studied his face, seeing my face is his. I even saw my eldest daughter's face in his. The hospital room was like the million others I'd been in: bed, vinyl floor, wood cabinets, a wood table and chair, a window overlooking businesses and green Atlanta country everywhere outside. My pops was hooked up to one of those machines that checked his vitals and beeped on and off. He was wearing a hospital gown, and I had on cargo shorts and a black T-shirt. My career in a place where I felt more powerful than ever, but I found myself looking over at my pops laid up looking more vulnerable than ever. My superhero laid in that hospital bed telling jokes and reminiscing. Our realities were two sides of a single coin.

"Man, you can go down there with them if you want to," Pops said. "I ain't about to die no time soon."

"You sure, Pop?"

"Yeah, I'm good man."

I felt like he was telling the truth. He had to be telling the truth. He had never lied to me before, why would he start? I hit my homies and told them I was coming. I grabbed my stuff and headed for the door. Right before I reached the door, Pops called my name:

"Epps!"

I turned around but didn't say anything.

"The dopeman my motherfucking role model," he said, with the biggest smile I'd ever seen on his face. I busted out laughing because around that time I had a song called "Role Model." The hook says, "The dopeman my motherfucking role model." The one thing about my pops is he had always supported my music, from the jump. I walked back over to his bed still laughing.

"Naw man you good," I told him.

He laughed, made a fist, and extended it my way. We pounded. He sat up and looked at me, face turned a bit more serious, more authority-like. More fatherly.

"Do it big, Epps," he ordered. "Do it big."

I drove to the show with a heavy heart. The entire trip was a blur, even the show. I was more subdued than normal. All I really thought about was getting through everything and getting back to Atlanta to hang out with my pops. But when I did get back, my pops was on a breathing machine. I was completely shocked. I had just been there six to eight hours before, giving pound with my pops, making jokes with my pops, and now he couldn't breathe on his own. I couldn't process it. The room that had been like every other hospital room suddenly wasn't. It seemed so silent. That bed that seemed like every other hospital bed took on a darker shade. The vinyl floors turned to quicksand, and I felt like I was sinking right into it. And the Atlanta country green outside the window looked lifeless. What the fuck happened so fast?

"What happened?" I asked the nurse.

"He started losing oxygen, and we had to provide him assistance."

"No no. We just spoke. I was just talking to him."

The breathing machine had his chest going in and out. He didn't look like my pops. He was just there, like that. No jokes, no laughing, no nothing. Just like that. And he stayed like that for about half the day.

I didn't leave his bedside. I talked to him, told old stories about the old house and police raids we overcame. I wanted him to know I was there. I didn't want him to feel alone like he had for so many years in prison. It's a hell of a thing to see your hero in that state. That breathing machine had tubes down my pops's throat. A person's natural reaction would be to pull the tubes out of their mouth.

That could be deadly. To prevent that from happening, they handcuffed my pops to the bed. My pops was fighting for his life in handcuffs like he had done so many times. He'd done years in prison, and here he was handcuffed again.

I can still see how he looked at me. He wanted me to do something. It was more than just him being uncomfortable, this was about dignity. His look said, *Epps, have these goddamn people take this shit out of my throat. Son, do something.* I had been accustomed to controlling things, fixing things, making things better. But there wasn't nothing I could do. I made them remove the handcuffs and when I did, he reached to pull the tubes out his mouth. They handcuffed him again. And once he was handcuffed a second time, he shot me the same *do something* look. I made them remove the handcuffs. When they did, he reached to pull the tubes out again. They handcuffed him a third time. This went on repeatedly.

The foundation was shaking. Just like it had so many times for us. All the times he was arrested in front of me. All the times his freedom was snatched. My pops was fighting for his life while being confined. His body wasn't working, and they wouldn't allow his hands to. I wanted to fix it. I needed to fix it. My pops expected me to fix it. I couldn't. I've heard all the stories about military torture: waterboarding, sleep deprivation, suffocation. If any of that shit looks like this, then it has to be hell. Because we were in hell. We were both suffering, repeatedly, and there was no end in sight.

The time moved slow, and then out of nowhere, he just started slipping. I'm still not exactly sure what happened but the emergency alert from the breathing machine went off, and panic completely took over. Nurses ran into the room and kicked me out. Everything and everybody was moving fast. Outside the room, there was a window I was able to look through to see inside. There was a lot of commotion. They used defibrillators to shock him back to life. He came back. That's when they allowed me back into the room, but not even two minutes later, it happened again.

The beeping started, and the nurses rushed back in. They made me leave the room, and I was looking through that window again, pleading with him, "Come on, Pop. Don't do me like that. You told me we were good. You said you were good." He came back again, and I went back in the room. But it kept happening. A third time, a fourth time. I was outside the room when one of the nurses walked up to me. I'll never forget what she told me: "Look, I lost my daddy also. But at this point, if he comes back, he'll be a vegetable. I understand why you don't want to let him go. But you have to let him go. We've already broken two ribs trying to bring him back, and if we are able to bring him back, he won't have the mind capacity to be anything." It was almost like the young doctor lady who I called out of her name had predicted all this. Maybe she had been right. Then I broke down. I broke down.

Before that moment, it had been forever since I'd cried. It's not like my pops told me not to cry, I just understood because he never did. I actually thought I was cried out. Think about our tear ducts being like windshield wiper fluid reservoirs. You know how it is when you click the windshield wiper fluid lever and nothing happens, or maybe just a small amount of fluid comes out? That's when you know you need more wiper fluid. My tear ducts had become like those reservoirs, and I think my reservoirs had been all out of fluid, or tears. I had been through so much in my life, cried so much as a kid, that I thought I had completely become numb to crying or feeling sad. My pops's circumstance proved to me that wasn't the case. When I came to terms that I really had to let him go, I just cried, and cried, and cried, and couldn't stop for a long time.

I'm an only child. My pops had been my main man through everything. He taught me how to be a man, how to stand tall. Without that guidance, I wouldn't be in the position I'm in now.

When he passed away, I was mad at everybody. I was mad at my mom for not staying with him at the hospital when I left to do the show. I was just upset.

The next couple of weeks were a blur. Everything reminded me of him. Everything still reminds me of him.

A few years ago, while getting busted pipes fixed in my basement, my plumber found a gift bag full of dollar bills. There were stacks of rolled-up dollar bills. Lots of them. I guess it was my pops's old stash he'd put away for a rainy day. I thought about him being at the house with the workers in the beginning when it was getting painted and updated. I wondered if that's when he made that his little stash spot. That's some shit my pops would've definitely done.

The one thing I'll remember more than anything else about him was his scent. He had a particular smell. Nothing musty or anything. He was definitely a very clean man. But he had a smell in his clothes, a fragrance. I still have one of his blue jean jackets and his smell is still on it.

And sometimes when that jacket is nowhere in sight, out of nowhere, I'll smell him. That's how I know he's around. That's when I know he's checking on me. That's what my intuition tells me. That's what my voice tells me. That's what God tells me. I can smell when Pops come around. It's a very familiar smell. It smells like God. It smells like love.

XIV

ONCE UPON A TIME IN CALI

As humans I believe we're already wired for survival. It's an instinct we're born with. Many times, without someone actually telling me to watch my back, I have felt that I might be in danger through my intuition. I have found myself in situations that might've cost me much more had I not been tapped into my voice. Had I not been connected enough to sense that something was off, I might've experienced some bad outcomes.

Remember in *The Matrix* when Neo saw the same black cat twice while they were walking up those stairs? He kind of started tripping and when Morpheus and Trinity asked him what was wrong, he mentioned something about déjà vu. Morpheus and Trinity then started to trip because they knew that if anyone experienced déjà vu, then that meant there was a glitch in the Matrix or that something in the Matrix had changed. Through trial and error, those two had become so tuned and tapped into understanding the Matrix that something seeming off would immediately alert them. The moment anything appeared or felt like it wasn't a part of the natural order, they'd get into survival mode. After Neo mentioned déjà vu, everyone prepared for conflict.

After all my years, life experiences, and trust in my intuition, I have come to a place where I can sense when something doesn't seem right.

By 2013, I had become a rap star. I was having my way, moving around, and also trying to introduce my people and the good people of Atlanta to as many experiences as I could. My entourage had been getting smaller, but my ideas had been getting bigger. When you first get on, you're often with a much larger entourage, but over time, your circle filters and slims down. Stuff happens, you know?

I was blowing up and moving around. I would do things to try and get the community out of Atlanta. I would try and get the hood out. I remember booking a big yacht in Miami. I set up a tour bus from Atlanta to Miami so that folks could jump on the yacht and do a twenty-four-hour kick-it thing. I probably had twenty-something people come down: We had food for everybody, drinks, and just offered a real authentic experience. Being generous and wanting to bring the hood out was very much a part of my character when I started. I was always trying to show people a good time or introduce them to something I had already done or been fortunate enough to be a part of.

The Cali trip was similar to that. I remember they had a place where you could actually smoke gas (weed) inside, a lounge. They had all these different kinds and flavors of weed. It may not sound like much today because gas is legal damn near everywhere and everything is different. But back then, that was unique. I remember thinking one day, *I have to get my guys up here, man.* I had been traveling, making money, and wanted to share the fruits of my labor with some of my good homeboys I hustled with. These were guys I had sold bags with, trapped with, and hung out with at 5540 Old National. I wanted to introduce them to something different.

I told them I knew a place that had some good gas, but they'd have to fly out to Cali to meet me. "I'm going to arrange everything," I told them. "I'll be coming from a show, but I'll meet y'all there." They were definitely down with the invitation. I knew the opportunity for them to get good gas would be something too good to pass up. I set it up for them to arrive on a particular day because I knew I'd be arriving in Cali from a show in Seattle the day after. So I flew the guys up.

Of the four homies I flew out to Cali, two had never been, which meant they had to turn up immediately. They hit up restaurants, bars, and dispensaries. The homies were eating good, drinking good, and smoking good. They had already been talking to the people I planned on introducing them to. They were moving around and waiting on me. I wasn't sure of everything they were getting into because I hadn't arrived yet.

Hearing bits and pieces about the good time they were having made me feel good. They were enjoying Cali, and that was exactly what I wanted for them. I wanted them to get out of Atlanta and catch some good West Coast vibes. By the time I landed, I was super excited to smoke and hang with the guys. I knew that if they were having a good time before I arrived, then they would really trip once they experienced the places I'd planned to take them to, both literally and medicinally. My plan was to show them a greater time, for us to smoke good and enjoy life.

I got off the plane super excited. I was with the same group that I'd normally travel with: deejay, two security folks (one who is my cousin), and a road manager. I decided to have my car service take me straight to the venue. I told the homies I'd meet them there.

The weather was nice, and while I don't remember the exact month, I'm pretty sure it was late spring. While we drove down the highway, I thought about 5540. All the good times I'd had with the guys I was getting ready to hang with. The closer we got to the venue, the crazier traffic got. This was downtown San Francisco in the middle of the day, so it all made sense. It might've been around 4 p.m. You had your suit-and-tie business folks, and then you had your regular folks who were just outside making it. There was a Four Seasons in the vicinity, all the typical big-city downtown surroundings.

Once we got close to the place where I was set to meet them, traffic really started to back up. I remember getting out the van maybe three storefronts away. I figured that was close enough. When I hopped out of the van, everybody hopped out and followed me. We started walking down the street, and as we walked, there were cars moving and horns blowing. There was also the stench of good gas. We were right there.

I still don't know what made me walk in front of everybody. That wasn't how we normally moved. I had security and everything. Usually, I walked more toward the back.

For some reason that day, I was leading the pack, like the natural leader I am. We were damn near right there when I noticed a car in front of the dispensary we were heading to. For some reason, *something told me* something was off. Right after that, a man got out the passenger seat and slid across the hood. Then, he started almost ducking down. It was definitely off. I remembered I had seen something like this in a movie. I don't remember what he looked like, or what he was wearing, I just know that my spidey-sense told me something wasn't right. We were in a crowded, well-lit area with people everywhere. He started crouching down, almost pretending like he was tying his shoe. *Something told me* it wasn't right, and right there in that moment, my body prepared for fight or flight. I didn't have time to alert my people like Morpheus and Trinity did, everything happened too fast. When I slowed down to really get a good look at the guy, he upped a firearm on me. "Here we go."

I busted a U-turn and started running before anybody else even peeped it, then they took off too. I ran through traffic but had no idea where I was going, I was just trying to get away from the threat. I didn't even look behind me, and I never heard the gun go off. Right after it felt like I had gotten away from the initial threat, another guy started running my way, almost as if they were doing a relay. This guy had a weapon too. I know the first guy didn't pass his gun like a baton, but that shit seemed that way. The second guy ran like he had some kind of training. He ran fast like a track star, like he had done this before. He ran with discipline and purpose, like it was a mission for him. All I could hope for was for it to be a simple robbery, but unlike the first guy, this motherfucker actually started shooting. *Boom, boom, boom.* I remember asking myself, "Is he shooting at me?"

Never in my life had I felt so defenseless. I didn't have a weapon because I had just gotten off a plane. I had no way to defend myself. I was out of town, didn't have a firearm on me, and didn't know karate. All the advantages were on his side. Things got worse when my pants started falling down. This was during the era of jean sagging, so I started holding my pants up as I was running. An easy mark. He was gaining on me, and everything seemed inevitable. I ducked, and when I did, I ended up falling to the ground. He ran up and stood directly over me. "Man, I don't even got nothing," I told him, trying not to look at his face, trying not to make eye contact. "I'm telling you, I don't got nothing."

I wasn't lying. I didn't have nothing but an American Express card in my wallet. I didn't have any cash or expensive jewelry. I didn't have nothing. He stood over me, not saying shit. He could've did me dirty. I thought he would. Then, I noticed him looking at my wallet chain. I was wearing a Versace belt, and a chain connected my Versace wallet to it. He snatched it off me and took off running down the street in broad daylight. I got up and dusted myself off, sat for a second, and reminded myself I wasn't dead. Then, not even a full minute after I watched him fleeing down the street I heard "Freeze." *Oh shit.* "Here we go again, again."

This time, it was the police.

"Freeze," one of the cops told me.

"Man, fuck all that." I was heated because I had been a second away from losing my life, and the cops had the nerve to run up and tell me to freeze. I started arguing with them.

"I'm the one that just got damn near assaulted. I'm not getting on no ground."

Then he instructed me not to move again, but he had changed his tone when he said it. He said it with concern. I complied, and when I did, he started to check me out.

"Aye man, I need you to sit down for a minute, you may be hit," he said.

"Naw, I don't think I'm hit."

"Your adrenaline could be running, and you just might not feel it. But you could be hit."

"Naw man. I think I'm good."

"We got an ambulance on the way. I'ma need you to get in the back of the ambulance."

"I don't want to get in the ambulance." I was shook up but had enough sense to worry about my business being all in the news. I could already imagine the headlines.

He was checking my head, then the weirdest thing happened. He pulled a bullet fragment out of my hair. A whole bullet fragment out of my fucking hair. It felt like a magic trick. You know how it goes when the magician touches somebody's ear and then pulls a quarter out? That's what it felt like. It felt like magic. I had been shot before, so I still didn't think I was shot. Nothing inside me was getting hot, and if you've ever been shot, you know that things inside you start to get hot. I haven't shared this story with too many people. The way I've dusted off and suppressed this trauma should be studied. The cop had pulled a bullet fragment out of my hair. I hadn't been hit though.

The van I had got out of had come back. My road manager got out the van crying, literally boohooing. He couldn't believe I was standing up. He couldn't believe I was on two feet. "Bro, I saw you when you got shot bro." He told me, "I saw you when you got shot." He was touching me, almost making sure I was real. He was hugging and grabbing me. I told him I was straight, but he was like, "Bro, I saw it. Naw man. Naw man. I saw you get shot." He couldn't control hisself. We hugged each other for a minute. I reassured him again that I was good. We stayed talking to the cops for a while, and then we left.

I went to the hotel, took a shower, and put some clothes on. I had a show in Oakland that night, which I decided to do. Nothing was going to stop me from doing that show. I had come too far, and was too turned up, to let a hater turn me down.

The show was at the Oracle Arena and ended up being one of the most lit shows I'd ever done in my life. The energy was just going crazy because I was happy to be alive. I'm not sure if I have ever felt more alive than I did performing that night. There were times onstage when I asked myself if I was almost in heaven. Maybe the show was some kind of holy waiting dimension before I crossed through the pearly gates. But I was very much alive, and my life would keep on moving. The next day, I shot the "Feds Watching" video at the Sheats-Goldstein Residence in LA with Pharrell Williams and wore all white.

Once upon a time in Cali, a nigga was shooting at me in broad daylight for, as far as I knew, nothing. For an American Express card and a Versace wallet. I'm thankful something kicked in before everything went down. My intuition and survival mode kicked in. While I do believe in déjà vu and its spiritual connections, it wasn't déjà vu that I felt before everything went down. It wasn't like Neo in *The Matrix*. There was no black cat to warn me, but I did feel something before the ambush happened and tapped into my need to survive. It had been written for me to be onstage later that night, to make it home to my loved ones, to continue my beautiful life. I'd like to thank those haters who tried blocking my destiny because I ended up giving the Bay one of the hardest shows they'd ever seen from me.

PART III

MUSCLE MEMORY

Before I go to work, let's get this straight. I am not Billy Eagle. I am plain Bill Eagle, giving all honor to God and the eagle. Since I know you so good, you can call me Red Eagle, or Bill Red Eagle. We are the Eagle family, as the female eagle is usually larger than her male counterpart, we eagles also carry their offspring as high as they can and then they drop them, because they know a real eagle can fly. Fly home my son. Soar to any height you desire. God is with you, and you have the wind beneath your wings. Say hello to my divine eagle. I hope she's doing good, and I know she's proud of you.

—Pops (through a prison letter)

XV

INVEST OVER IMPRESS

Being intuitive, or instinctive, is like having something that you can't really understand, or articulate to someone to help them understand. There's no definitive way to articulate it when you come equipped with these senses, this ability to be tuned and tapped into your intuition and inner voice. Having this knowledge, or this conscience, this voice, has helped me navigate through business and relationships, personal and professional, both inside and outside my music career. It's given me game. *Game.* That's a loaded word with slightly different interpretations depending on how you're using it. It's been used in many regions and traps for quite some time. I heard it growing up and still hear it almost every day.

Here's the thing: I'm not talking about game, like "playing a game," or sports. I'm talking about how a person approaches life, how somebody's mind, principles, and integrity works. Wisdom. The way a person moves in the world and understands the world around them. The rules of life, relationships, neighborhoods, and the order of things. That kind of game.

Game can't be easily explained. Like with most Black vernacular, it doesn't have a neat definition. Game is mostly undefinable, but you know it when somebody's putting you up on it, putting you up on game. Have you ever found yourself in a conversation with somebody or a group of people who knew a lot more about a particular topic than you? And the longer the conversation continued, the more you started taking mental notes to make sure you'd have the information just in case you ever found yourself in that conversation again? That's called being put on game.

This is about anytime you receive information that makes your life more holistic, more well-rounded. Many people have put me on game in my life, and I've put people on game. I'm a student of life, and I'm always looking to learn. Information has always been key to my success. Oftentimes we might pretend to know something we don't because we don't want to come off naïve or uninformed. That's never been my approach. If there's something I don't understand or know enough about, I'm either going to ask questions or do my own research. Doing your own research is putting yourself up on game. You can't just wait for someone to put you on game, sometimes you need to do it yourself. You understand what I'm saying? You understand what I just did here? Put you on game.

I first started getting into real estate many years ago because my mother was a loan officer. She would put me on the game of how real estate worked. She did this sometimes by having direct conversations with me, and other times, I just watched how she worked and listened to her conversations with other people. I was even a student in my own home. It only made sense that I would invest in real estate once I grew up and felt ready. I always believed in having various streams of income, even when I was trapping. My entrepreneurial journey started with selling real estate. I bought properties without really knowing what to do with them. I was just hoarding them. Would buy them and just have them.

My first investments were some apartment buildings off Metropolitan, near the Pittsburgh area. Pittsburgh is a historic Black working-class neighborhood in Atlanta. It was a great place for me to start and get my hands dirty. I continued buying properties for many years; some were more successful than others. The more years I spent in real estate, the more game I learned.

The more game I learned, the more I experienced financial gain. One of my more successful properties was on Peters Street. I actually purchased three properties on Peters Street around 2014. One of those ended up being inquired about by a young lady named Snoop who was already running a hospitality space. Her business was doing very well, which made an impression on me. Running a successful business is not easy. There are a million things to worry about and a billion things to stay on top of. When I interviewed Snoop, she explained to me that she needed more space, and after seeing her PNLs, I knew she was about her business.

When I first met Snoop, we introduced ourselves, and then went over all the particulars of her renting the place from me. We discussed things like how much I would charge for rent, when the place would be available, and all the other ins and outs. What I remember most was that she had a certain kind of glow, a certain vibe, a certain energy. It was my first time meeting her, but she felt familiar. She told me about her restaurant and how long she'd been in business. She also talked about a lot of new hospitality ideas she had. I remember her discussing serving specialty drinks in mason jars. That sounded really artistic and stood out to me. As an artist a lot of what I do is concept-driven, so I respected her ideas on running a business.

She told me about herself and gave me a little background information. In that very moment, *something told me* that this person could be a valuable asset to me and my brand, someone to help me manifest new ideas I had been thinking about. I had already been thinking about opening up a restaurant lounge kind of place. I had just been too busy up to that point to get things started. Meeting Snoop that day felt like a sign and opportunity to get things in motion. And not only was my mind telling me that, but my intuition was telling me that. My intuition was putting me on game.

In his book *Decisive Intuition: Use Your Gut Instincts to Make Smart Business Decisions,* business coach and author Rick Snyder says, "Intuition is about your relationship with yourself first and then about your relationship with others and the environment at large. It's about learning your own rhythms and signals for when something feels off or right on the money. Learning to trust your intuition is the greatest gift you can give yourself. It makes the difference in business decisions, and it enables you to have a purposeful, fulfilling life. And it just feels good to trust yourself once you've cultivated a relationship with your intuition."

By 2014, I had developed a strong trust in my intuition, my inner voice. I know how to put things together and how to put people together. I knew Snoop was somebody I wanted to work with, even if we had just met that afternoon. I knew her business acumen in hospitality mixed with my marketing, business savvy, and charm would make some millions.

We became business partners that day and immediately put the wheels in motion for a brand that many people today know as Esco. Esco started out as a restaurant lounge in Atlanta nine years ago but has grown since.

We now have four franchises and a couple more opening soon. This all came from that gut feeling I had when I first met Snoop. I like to think of myself as a talent scout. I can meet somebody and form a general opinion about them. I say "opinion" because it's not based on facts. It's based on impression and my own subjective deductions, which I'm cool with. My deductions are informed by my intuition and inner voice, and it has never steered me wrong. When I met Snoop, I saw a kindred spirit and hustler. That same day I went into business with a complete stranger. I didn't know her from a can of paint. That's crazy, right?

We have soared since then, and made millions based on my gut feeling, my intuition. The voice in my head said, *Aye man let's try it. Trust this person. You can believe in her spirit.* Being able to scout and feel someone that's passionate about a certain thing has worked for me and helped me navigate my business. I can't work with someone who isn't passionate about their craft.

Everyone I do any kind of work or business with is passionate. My manager is passionate, my doctor is passionate, my barber is passionate, my mechanic is passionate, my landscaper is passionate, my son's coach is passionate, my realtor is passionate, my chef is passionate, my workout buddies are passionate, my dancers at Candyland are passionate, the music artists I work with are passionate, the visual artists who design my cover art are passionate, the engineer I work with almost daily is extremely passionate. Nolan has been my engineer for the past seven or eight years. He basically lives with me. I've come a long way from the days of needing permission for studio time. I have invested in my own studio, I have my own engineer, and whenever I want to work, we work. We plug in, load it up, and make it happen.

I think investing became the norm for me because I come from a gambling background, and investing is the closest thing to gambling I can think of. Sometimes you win, a lot of times you lose. I remember when I was introduced to Rashaun Williams. He started the Queensbridge Venture Partners fund a long time ago with Nas. He came to my office years ago and met with my team and actually tried to get me to start my own VC fund. Prior to that, I had invested in a couple of properties I thought were reasonable and smart decisions to make to try and rehab. Rashaun and I became cool, and we're still cool.

I build relationships one person at a time. Every person I meet might be an opportunity to do some business. I don't look down on nobody, and I definitely don't worship nobody. I meet people where they are, and like the great Maya Angelou once said, "When someone shows you who they are, believe them the first time." Our poet mother was giving us game.

I've built many more relationships through investing. I now have a Smoothie King in State Farm Arena with my guy Phillip. I've known Phillip a long time. He had his own Smoothie King that I used to go to, and I remember telling him, "This is very much organic and a part of my lifestyle. One day I want to get me a Smoothie King." He said, "Shit, I'll partner up with you." It happened just that fast.

Our first one had to be in the State Farm Arena where the Atlanta Hawks play because I'm Toni, I'm 2 Chainz, everything I do is big. Our Smoothie King is doing very well. But even when investing, I'm listening to the voice in my head: *Should I do this, should I not do this? Is this the way to go? Should I vet this person? Should I vet that process?* Sometimes you can be spontaneous and make the wrong decision, and sometimes being spontaneous can help you make the right decision. Listening to your inner self will always assist you in making the best decision.

I've invested in other businesses too. I have a vegan pizza restaurant, Pizza Verdura. I opened that with my guy David, a Jewish fella who's really passionate about getting his healthy produce out. We have worked hard and made sure to separate ourselves from any other vegan spot. The mission of Pizza Verdura is very much a part of my organic lifestyle. (More on food later.) The restaurant is also something I believed would make my portfolio look more colorful. It's going very well. A couple business ventures I've done with Rashaun have been up and down. Some are going very well, some are not. But it's ongoing and it's something that's very much a part of my lifestyle. As a businessman and an artist, I understand that no artist can become a billionaire without investing in businesses or coming up with products. That's my thinking behind my business energy. I'm always thinking of how to hit that next lick. You peeping game?

My most sincere blessing and investment has been my kids. I love my kids. I love my wife. I love my mom. I love my life. Investing in my wife and us having kids has built my foundation. I put every financial, emotional, and spiritual resource I have in all of my kids, and I pray they will reach their full potential. I make sure to put time into my children. The money has been good their entire lives, but I make sure they have experiences they can lean back on.

I remember experiences more than I remember my account balance. I'm always trying to do something with my kids. Take them traveling, to a game, introduce them to interesting people. Whether it makes sense to them now, I hope it will in the future. My kids have been all over the globe; they've had their feet on the hardwood and watched Trae Young go for forty. My children are full of life and experiences. I made it cool to sit courtside with your kids at NBA games. Everybody used to have an entourage with them courtside. We had to switch that up. Ain't nothing doper than being courtside with your kids and sharing that experience with them. The ones you live with and do life with. Good memories with the people you love stay forever. On any given day, I can remember every single moment with my pops, all of his investments in me. You dig what I'm saying? Fathers, lean in. I'm putting you on game.

Not too long ago, I went to Eliantte to look at some jewelry. I was close to buying this really nice expensive chain. My intuition told me, *For the same price the jeweler is about to charge for the chain, you could expand your business brand*. And like I always do, I listened. I used the money I was about to spend on that chain to invest in Pizza Verdura. Full circle.

To be clear, I had the money to do both, but I already have so many chains, what or who am I trying to impress by buying another? I don't think you can ever have enough businesses.

Something told me, "Don't do that, do this." And now I'm a business owner, a business partner. I had to grow into this mentality, had to grow into trusting my business gut. In the past, I would've definitely wanted to put that shine on. You see it, you buy it, you wear it. It has that instant gratification. That's not how owning a business works. It could be anywhere from three to five years before you see a profit or get that gratification.

It's not instant. I'm trying to put you on game. You dig? I could've gotten the chain, or I could've done both. I've chosen to have smarter resolutions and earnings that rest and grow. A business investment is impressive but not something you can show people right away. A lot of my entrepreneurship is based off organic connections, my being an organic individual.

In addition to Esco restaurant lounges (in Atlanta, Columbus, Dallas, and Memphis), Smoothie King, and Pizza Verdura, I also own Candyland, a swanky Atlanta strip club. I've invested in ZenWTR and Instacart. I am a business. All these business opportunities happened organically and mean plenty to me. But no material investment has meant more than the houses I've been able to buy my mama. No property, restaurant, chain, watch, or car has meant more than handing over house keys and reminding her that "God is love."

XVI

IDEAS ARE CURRENCY

I've been in the music business for a long time. I've been grinding, working, really trying to make it for almost two decades. In the beginning, I would just put out mixtapes and build relationships with people to try to make things better for me and my family.

I built a lot of relationships through selling weed. I actually sold weed to a lot of artists who came to Atlanta wanting to get high. Ludacris would make the connections because he worked on the radio. Anytime somebody came to town looking for weed, he would point them in my direction. I served and met a lot of people in the music industry before I even started to really take music seriously. Never would I approach them like, "I spit, I got bars." It never happened like that. It was really about the relationships.

This one particular time, a long time ago, I was at Patchwerk, the iconic recording studio in Atlanta. Back then, I would use my hustling money to book studio time at well-known studios where I knew a bunch of big artists would be. That was my way of getting in. Maybe I might run into them in the bathroom, or cross paths in the hallway.

During my session at Patchwerk, I was working in the "B" room, and in the "A" room, which is the bigger room, Cash Money Records had a session going on. This is right after B.G. had gone away, and they were reorganizing Cash Money Records with Wayne. I was rapping in my session and then somebody came in and asked me if I had some weed. I was like, "Yeah, I always keep a little weed on me." They invited me into the "A" room, and that's basically how I met Baby from Cash Money.

That day was the start of my becoming a part of the family. When I went over to their session, Baby was not smoking at the time, he was more of a drinker. I watched how he looked out for everybody in the studio. Plenty of food was ordered to make sure everybody was fed. I'm talking about all kinds of Chinese food, pizza, big boxes of chicken. Everybody was going to eat. I gave him two zips of weed. At that time, zips were $450 apiece. I remember him telling me, "Say Slim, I'ma get you, ya know." I said, "Okay. No problem."

Another time he asked if I knew how to get to the mall. I'll never forget the white conversion van he was driving. He would literally drive the whole crew around. I told him how to get to South DeKalb Mall, and I ended up going with them.

We pulled up to the mall and went into this fashion store. All the guys were in there just going crazy. They were picking up stuff, trying on stuff. I was just sitting there chilling. Baby told me, "Slim, you don't want to get nothing?" I was like, "Naw, I'm cool." Then one of the guys walked up on me like, "Boy, you better get something. Boy, you are tripping." I was watching dudes take off the clothes they walked in with and just leave them. Everybody was walking out in new clothes.

At some point I decided to grab a pair of Timberlands. I figured, might as well. Baby paid for the Timberlands, and I remember thinking, *Damn, my pops ain't even did nothing like that for me in a minute.* The guys were heading back to New Orleans later that night. Baby still had a nine-hundred-dollar tab for the weed I'd given him. I had been appreciative of all the relationship building we had been doing, but I needed the nine hundred. When he was like, "We're going to New Orleans tonight," my thought became, *Shit, I guess I'm going too because I'm going to get this money.*

We went down there, and he had this big Cash Money mansion with a jacuzzi in the middle. Everybody was playing video games and kicking it. There was a lot of people around, some I knew and others I didn't. I remember Mack 10 being around. I remember a bunch of Bloods being around. There were a lot of red cars around. This was back when they had the stretch PT Cruisers. I had been just kind of hanging, peeping everything, and that's actually when I met Wayne. He came over to the house, and me and him linked up and smoked some real good pressure. That started our long-term friendship.

During that time, I had been messing with this producer that me and Dolla had found. When Dolla and I had the group Playaz Circle, we went to a beat-making competition in Birmingham. I had been in the bathroom in this little club, and I heard this beat. I walked out of the bathroom, and the producer ended up being this guy M16. I introduced myself and we started working together. He was nice with the beats. When it came time to do a beat, he would ask me to describe the beat I wanted. He would ask me about the vibe, the sound, the feeling. That's not as easy as people think. It's not easy to describe the beat you're looking for, and it damn sure ain't easy to make a beat that somebody is describing to you. Around the end of 2006, Hov had this song, "Show Me What You Got." I really liked the beat on that song, so I told M16 to make a beat like that but to add organs. I told him to put some Pimp C in it. He went to his shed and made the beat I described. That's how we got the "Duffle Bag Boy" beat.

At this time, my current studio, Street Execs, which I'm part owner of, was owned by T.I. Wayne had been in the studio working, and that day I went to Lenox Square to do some shopping. I have always been into fashion (more on this in a couple chapters): Gucci, Louie, Prada, Bally. I have always been one of those guys. I was looking at shoes in one particular store, and they brought out these red Guccis with the fur on the inside. I thought to myself, *Damn, I got to get these for shawty.*

Wayne used to wear Supras, these like skate shoes. He actually got me into wearing them. But I knew he would love the red Guccis, so I ended up getting them. I brought the shoes to the studio that day and gave them to him. I also brought the CD with M16's beat on it to him, too. I give him the shoes, the beat, and went about my business. I remember little Peewee being in the studio too that day. It was a good vibe up in there.

Time went on, and me and Wayne continued to develop a great relationship. Baby's house that I went to about a year ago with the jacuzzi had been flooded by

Katrina. The whole neighborhood and most of New Orleans was underwater. Wayne and Baby had to move from Louisiana to Miami.

When they got to Miami, Wayne had hit me like, "Come on down and fuck with me." I was definitely with it. I booked my flight and headed down. *Something told me* to do that. As soon as I landed, Cortez picked me up in a Maserati. He was driving, and Wayne was in the front seat. I sat in the back. It was just us three. We headed straight to the mall. Prada was hot at the time. We went to a shoe store, and Wayne being the player that he is, bought him a pair of shoes. He then went over to the wall of Pradas and bought the whole wall in both his size and mine. He was like, "Gimmie all of them." While we we're waiting for them to bring the Pradas out the back, he asked me, "What you think about that song I did for you? The hook." I said, "What hook?" I had no idea what he was talking about. He said, "Tez [Cortez], what did you do with that song?" Tez said he emailed it to me. I was so confused. I asked, "What email?" Tez told me the email address, but it wasn't the right one. He had sent the song to somebody else. I was like, "That ain't my email," and they were like, "Ah shit."

In the middle of the store, Wayne started using his hands to make the beat on his chest. He started trying to remember the hook: "*If I don't do nothing, I'ma ball. I'm counting all day like the clock on the wall.*" But he couldn't remember the rest. I couldn't believe it. The small part of the hook he remembered was fire, and the whole time the recording had been sitting in an inbox that wasn't mine. Wayne could tell I was feeling it, and was like, "Fuck it.

We're going to the studio." We left the mall and went right to the studio.

When we got there, he played me the song with the hooks on it, "Duffle Bag Boy." He played the song, and I told him, "Dang, that's hard. You did that for me, bruh?" And he was like, "Yeah."

What I heard felt like a hit. I had never had one before, but I knew the song was different. And I knew people was definitely going to fuck with it.

I went into a different room and called Dolla. I told Dolla, "We got one. Bruh, we got one." He was like, "What? We got one what?" I didn't even have it on CD at the time. They gave me the hard drive of what Wayne had done. I went back to Atlanta a couple days later, not really remembering everything that happened in Miami, but remembering the feeling of knowing that I was coming back home with a hit in my pocket.

I remember calling everywhere to get studio time. Like I mentioned in an earlier chapter, we were signed to DTP and would need to book time through Luda's team. The first time I called to book time, they said not today. But the next time I called, they let me come over, and I played the song. Everybody agreed the song was hard. I had done my part. I remember Luda's manager, Chaka, saying something that caught Dolla's attention. He said, "This your man, right? Why is he talking about little duffle bag boys?" The way he said it made it seem like Wayne was trying to peewee us out on the hook. I remember thinking, *How a dude gonna do a song for me, do a favor for me, and then diss me on the song?* I didn't feel that way about the hook. I disagreed.

Dolla, on the other hand, was like, *fuck you, fuck Wayne, fuck everybody*. He agreed with Chaka and didn't want to do the song. He left. Before he did, I was trying hard to persuade him to do it. I was like, "Bro, you need to do this. We about to be gone. We about to be up." Ironically, Luda said he'd do it, but I believed I could eventually get Dolla to do it. He had to. It was going to be Playaz Circle's first hit. Me and Dolla had been through too much not to do the song together. Dolla ended up doing the song.

"Duffle Bag Boy" became a hit, fast. Wayne went on tour and called me to see if I wanted to go on tour with him. I used my own money to join him on that tour. My voice told me to take that opportunity. I ended up building a tighter relationship with Wayne and Young Money, the whole family. That's how we got cool. That's how we became family.

When I got off the tour, I got back to 5540 and, like I mentioned, stopped selling packs cold turkey. I ended up doing a mixtape called *T.R.U. REALigion*. After that dropped, I started getting so many opportunity calls from so many different people and artists. When it was time to start my own label, I couldn't think of anything else but T.R.U. It always had a deep meaning for me. T.R.U. The Real U. My voice was telling me that no matter what I did in my career, I had to make sure I stayed true to myself. I had to get down to the nitty-gritty of who I was and what I represented. I knew the industry was full of fakes, full of vultures. I had to protect my integrity and authenticity at all costs.

I want to speak on T.R.U., the record label I have. The acronym T.R.U. means "The Real U." Not to be confused with the legendary TRU No Limit, which I'll get to because I have had to educate some on how I would never take anyone else's idea, or anybody else's identity.

T.R.U. came along with the rise of 2 Chainz. From Tity Boi's transition to 2 Chainz, many things happened. Relationships, traveling, shows, and countless radio interviews. During the rise of 2 Chainz as my rap name and brand, I wore a lot of True Religion, the clothing company. I'm not sure exactly what it was about True Religion, I just liked the way the jeans dripped. I was wearing True Religion all the time.

After one long flight, while the plane was landing, I came up with a concept. What *true* meant to me. I broke it down to mean "the real you." Normally when I get off a plane I go straight to the bathroom. We wanted to re-create that moment since the idea came to me on a plane. We ended up doing a photo shoot at Lenox Square prior to its closing. The picture was of me at a urinal, my Louis Vuitton carry-on at my side, and the True Religion logo on the back pocket of my pants. That photo became the cover for my world-renowned mixtape *T.R.U. REALigion*. T.R.U. "Real" "Ligion." The study of being real or solid. I'm not talking about the "I'm a real nigga" cliché, but about honoring how we can be real and true to ourselves.

Over the years I have incorporated TRU into my raps and used "TRU" as an ad-lib. When I signed it under my own company, I was honestly happy and still am happy in my own skin and able to look in the mirror and be thankful for what God has created. I'm thankful for where I've come from, where I've been, and where I'm going. I never took anything from anybody. I am one of the most creative human beings God has put on this earth. As a matter of fact, I still have ideas. I'm sure people might say, "We all have ideas." But we all don't understand the power of a good idea. People buy ideas, people steal ideas, not me. I come up with my own ideas every day and it feels great.

As a matter of fact, ideas are currency. And let me tell you, I'm rich as a motherfucker, man. I have my own ideas, my own identity. When I think about the real me, I think about that voice in my head, my soul, my spirit. Everything that's created this human being is the real me. I hope you're the real you too, because as they say, and we know it's a cliché, everybody else is taken.

XVII

I CAN FEEL EYES

When I think about my voice or being intuitive, I think about the times when I can actually pick up the phone or not pick it up and know what the conversation is going to be about. I can anticipate what a person is going to talk about or would've talked about. For example, one time my phone was going crazy, and when I picked it up, it was my homeboy on the other end. He had previously called me so many times that I started praying. I started praying by like the fifth time he called. "Man, I hope everything is alright with my boy."

Sure enough, when I called him back, he said to me, "They killed little one. They killed my son." I'll never forget it. This was my homeboy since the ninth grade. We had been cool for so long that he had become family. I actually remembered when his son's mother was pregnant with him. That's how long we'd been close. And I just remember that day. I wanted my intuitive feeling to be off. I wanted my conscience to be wrong so freaking bad. I just wanted to be wrong. But I wasn't, and my intuition and spirit were speaking so loud to me that I just knew something was wrong.

I remember another time when I was away from home working. I had to be sleeping hard because I hadn't heard my phone ringing. My security came into my room and told me that my wife had been trying to get ahold of me. I called my wife back, but prior to calling her back, I just knew there was going to be some bad news. I started praying, hoping that everything was okay, not wanting to hear any bad news. I prayed that all my loved ones were okay and that everything back home was under control. Sure enough, when I called my wife back, she told me my homeboy Johnny had passed away. I was devastated. That was my partner, man, I loved that dude. I really loved that nigga. A real good friend and he's definitely missed.

Sometimes being intuitive has its ups and downs. Being so connected to the source comes with responsibility. I really believe that we can sense things. You can, with intuition, create a stronger sense of self. I challenge everyone to try and find that connection.

Try and find your Wi-Fi connection with the higher power. That connection is one of the reasons I believe I've been so successful. I actually listen to my voice; I listen to my conscience. I follow my guidance, which has led to me following my dreams. I follow the spirit. For someone who's never thought like this, it can sound weird, unbelievable, or unrelatable. But I feel like we should do whatever works for us.

I want to challenge everyone to locate and trust their deep inner connections. I can promise you that your life will expand in the most positive ways. "Intuition should be an integral part of your life, like exercise or meditation.

Employing it will open you up and add to the quality of both your thinking and your emotional selves," writes author Laura Day in her book *Practical Intuition*.

Day calls intuition a sixth sense and says, "You use your five primary physical senses—touch, sight, smell, hearing, taste—to gather information about the world around you. . . . The key difference is that intuition perceives things *without reliance on senses*. Intuition is nothing more than a process of gaining information that does not rely on your senses, your memory, your experience, your feelings, or your other thought processes." It's trusting your gut.

Intuition is a very strong tool you can use to learn more about yourself. It is really accurate. I can see someone from across the room, male or female, and depending on the setting, I may not be able to speak with them in that moment. Maybe the only thing we're able to do is give each other a nod. There've been a lot of times when something tells me I'm supposed to connect with a certain person at a certain moment. That me and that person should connect and talk.

I might see fifty people at any given event but know I'm supposed to connect with one in particular before I leave. A lot of times, before the night is over, I'll run into that person and have a dope conversation with them. Whenever this happens, those conversations seem important or meaningful. It might be about business opportunities or something else. Either way, when I feel my intuition guiding me to connect with a certain person, I listen. I've mentioned in previous chapters all the industry opportunities that have come my way through me listening to my voice and making good connections.

Recently, I took my son Halo to a Falcons game. We were watching the Falcons from the field; the Chiefs had come to town. Me and Halo had just done a podcast with Kyle Pitts, the standout tight end for the Falcons. Pitts was on the field, and me and Halo were off to the side. At some point, Halo started yelling out to Pitts, like, "Yo, Kyle. Yo, Kyle." It didn't seem like Kyle heard him because he didn't look in our direction.

Right after that, I started staring at Kyle for a minute, you know, really putting my eyes on him. The stadium guy that had walked us down asked if we were ready to go back up. The players were about to go to the locker room and get ready for the game. I told the stadium guy we were ready to go back up and get to our seats before the team headed to the locker room and the pregame festivities started. The way we were positioned on the field, if we didn't get out of the way before the players walked back to the locker room, we'd have to wait until they walked past.

We started making our way to our seats, but didn't make it far enough in time and had to wait for the players, we had to stay in one spot. We hadn't even been standing there a minute before Kyle came walking past. In a crowd of people, he looked right over at me and Halo and said, "What up." He didn't hear Halo yelling his name earlier, but once I laid eyes on him, I knew we'd connect before I left Mercedes-Benz Stadium with my son.

Man, I'm so connected to the source that I can actually walk into an arena where I'm not performing and feel when someone or people are looking at me. If I'm onstage of course I feel everybody watching me. But I'm saying I can go to an event, party, club, lounge, and feel when I'm being watched. Not just when I walk in.

When I walk in, of course people will look at me, or watch me 'cause I'm tall, and I'm me. I'm saying I can be in a place for thirty minutes or an hour and feel somebody from clear across the room watching me. I can feel eyes. I can actually feel eyes. I can feel when eyes are on me. Whether or not I catch them looking at me, I can feel it. I might turn around and see a young lady smiling, waving, "What's up, shawty." Mind you, nobody else in her area is even looking in my direction. I might turn another way and see a guy in the corner saluting me, "I like what you doing, man. Much respect." I can feel those things. I can feel eyes. Dr. Bradley Nelson calls thoughts energy in his book *The Emotion Code*. He says, "This doesn't mean that we can read other people's minds, but the energy of other people's thoughts *is* detected to some degree on a subconscious level. Try staring intently at the back of someone's head in a crowd, and inevitably they will turn and look right at you before long. Lots of us have had this experience; if you haven't, try it. It works every time!"

I think this is being tapped into the energy around you, the frequencies around you. Being someone that's in the streets and conscious of everyone from the feds to the robbers, this empathic sense has served me. We can actually feel when certain things are getting close to us. Not just physically, but when a certain energy is getting close to us.

It could be that you're under investigation. Or you might sense you're being targeted for a setup or armed robbery. These antennae came up very early for me in the streets, and I could always feel who was looking at me and if they possessed positive or negative light when I walked into a room. I've been able to use that, bottle it, and take it with me on my journey to adulthood, to manhood. I'm able to go to a game and sit on the wood. I'm able to meet a billionaire businessman who says he's been watching me for a year, or someone who says, "I've been watching you bring your kids to the game since they were little, and I like how you move." I can feel when a person has their phone camera out getting ready to take a picture of me and thinks I'm unaware. That's when I look over in their direction and smile. "Hi. I knew you were there. I felt that. I felt you."

XVIII

IF I DIE, BURY ME INSIDE THE LOUIE STORE

In the seventh grade, I went to Gresham Park Elementary School. I was staying in Decatur at the Misty Waters Apartments off Candler Road and took the bus to school. I used to get fresh on Fridays. Every Friday, I would wear the same red polo. It was long sleeve with the navy blue man. Polo was my thing. I only had two of them at the time, but the red one was my favorite. I felt invincible when I wore that damn shirt. I'd mix up the pants a little bit. I might go khaki, might go blue jean. No matter what else was going on with my outfit, I was coming with that red motherfucker every Friday.

I used to look at my peers like, "What the hell y'all wearing? Y'all shirts got collars all bent up, old bacon-neck-ass collars." Not me. I had to be fresh. This was around the time I started getting more into fashion and how clothes made me feel.

I used to lay out my clothes the night before. Whenever

summer break was almost over, man, the first day of school couldn't come quick enough for me. I'd spend the summer stacking up on clothes, knowing I was about to put some stuff together once the school year started.

I was a hustler when it came to getting new clothes. I'd go around to my grandmother's house and try to get them to buy me some shoes. Then, I'd hit up my uncle and have him buy me a coat. Putting different arrangements together and making it all work was the fun part. I would just make things work and piece outfits together. Your average person might see a certain shirt, pants, shoes, but not fully imagine how they could work together because they don't naturally blend.

Me, even in the seventh grade, I could see an outfit coming together in my mind before trying the clothes on. Fashion is very much a part of who I am. My seventh-grade fashion sensibility has stayed with me. Today, I pick my outfits out depending on where I'm performing, whether it's Vegas or Chicago. I know what a Houston vibe should feel like, I know what a Miami vibe should feel like. I pick out my shoes depending on how long I'll be onstage. It's a whole thing with me. It's a culture. Fashion is my armor, it's my energy. It's my charge, it's my reset.

My voice often tells me what to put on. But it's so tricky sometimes because man, I'll try and outsmart some shit, try to teach people about how this fashion thing works without hurting them too hard. I really be wearing shit according to the region I'm in, the city I'm in, and the size of the show. Say, for instance, I'm set to perform in a city that don't have a Balenciaga store. I would probably wear some Balenciaga because I know they can't get it there. Wherever I go, I'm going to come with something hard, and sometimes I do go over-the-top. I'm always going to push the envelope.

I definitely dress according to what day of the week it is. My whole process is voice-based, down to the cologne I put on. I have never just put on any cologne for any reason. I'm not lazy like that. It all has to come from inspiration and be thought out. The clothes I wear are a representation of me and how I prefer to introduce myself to the world around me.

I literally see my closet in my head before I even get to it. The voice in my head is like, *You can get that, and then you take that and put that with that.* It's really crazy. Even when it comes to my wardrobe person who shops for me. I tell him, "You didn't see that, did you? You didn't know I was coming like that, did you?" And he'll be like, "Hell naw. I didn't even see that pairing together like that." Everything be thought out, felt out, and strategic.

Just tonight, the Hawks played the Pistons at State Farm Arena. I threw on Louie jeans with Louie shoes and a Supreme shirt with the Hawks jacket. I liked my outfit, but I do have better Louie. I went soft Louie tonight. I went light Louie. I went diet Louie. My voice told me I didn't need to really put on like that for the game. I knew I was going to be seen either way, but every fashion situation is different. I had already expected there would be empty seats before getting to the game. My voice told me what kind of vibe it would be. No disrespect, but had the Hawks been playing the Lakers, I would've worn something different.

Let's say I'm attending a Lakers-Warriors game. That's gone be different. When I go to a game like that, I'll probably have on seven, eight, nine, or even ten thousand dollars' worth of clothes. It depends on the team. It's that well thought out. I never wake up and think, *Let me just wear this today*. No, it's more thought out and more of a feel thing. I have plenty of clothes. I probably have eight closets in different states. I have one in Florida, five in Atlanta, and two in LA. I can see them all in my head down to each rack. I have Balenciaga racks, Bottega racks, Prada racks, Gallery racks, Rick Owens racks. The list goes on. At any given time, I can see every detail in every closet. I can see everything that's in all of them shits, even when I'm not there.

I remember early in my career I had to do New York Summer Jam for Hot 97. If you don't know anything about Summer Jam, it's a big event. Thousands of people, huge stage. I love being onstage, it's my comfort zone. It's one of the most comfortable places for me. I remember doing interviews in the back before the show. I was getting into my zone, getting geared up to put on a great performance.

One of the guys who worked for the label came in and said, "Chainz," and then I thought I heard him say, "It's about fifteen thousand people out there." I was like, "Okay, cool." When I went out there to do the show, I could tell there wasn't fifteen thousand people. I was pissed. After the show, I got offstage and the same guy was like, "Yo, what did you think, man?" I was like, "I'm mad as hell." He was like, "Why you mad? I thought it sounded great." I said, "Because I thought you said fifteen thousand people was out there, but it was really more like fifty thousand. Had I'd known that, I would've worn a different outfit."

I can turn my fashion up or down at any point. Even my turn down is calculated. My son may have a basketball game, and my inner dialogue might say, *It's gone be some parents and hardworking folks up in there. Don't go in there creating too much distraction.* For something like that, I might wear some Halo Ones and a Nike Tech. Definitely sleeves long enough to cover all my expensive-ass bracelets. I rarely take my bracelets off. I actually sleep with them. My airport attire is dressed down, but it's a different kind of dressed down. At the airport, I never know who I might run into or how much time I might have to sleep on the plane. I might do something like Balenciaga nylons with the all-black hoodie, mask, black Balenciaga shades, and comfortable shoes.

I save big outfits for big events like award shows, the Super Bowl, and All-Star weekend. It gets so serious, man. When I go to a gym, I actually try and be one of the bummiest, non-matching, mix-matched-wearing persons in there. People will literally come up to me like, "Is that you? You 2 Chainz? Man, you can't be. I ain't never seen you look like this." People will be in there with their matching Nike and Under Armour tech shit on. Not me, I'm in the gym mix-matching. It gives me a good excuse to lock into my workout and not interact too much with the public. "I'm just working out, man. I don't even normally take pictures looking like this. I'm just trying to be low-key." I might even wear pajama pants. I ain't playing. I don't care about my shoes. Might have on some basic Yeezys or Nike Vapors. Something unassuming. My buddies I work out with usually have on matching neon tops and bottoms. I'm not coming like that to the gym. I could if I wanted to. I don't want to.

In terms of fashion, my intuition plays a role in who I work with, collaborate with, share my ideas with. Upon meeting Ye, we would talk on the phone for hours, just getting to know each other. We had so many things in common, and when I eventually started working with GOOD Music, he brought in a lot of resources to help me bring my dreams and goals to fruition. Some of the people Ye brought to the table were Virgil Abloh, Matthew Williams, Jerry Lorenzo, and a bunch of other guys.

I remember going to brainstorm in a room with everyone and there were a bunch of symbols on the wall. It almost looked like hieroglyphics. That's how it looked. There were all these different symbols and explanations of what they meant. The wall also had all these iconic album covers. I remember we just talked about what we were going to do for my first album cover (*Based on a T.R.U. Story*). It was like a creative think tank kind of meeting. At some point, Virgil pulled out Bruce Springsteen's *Born in the U.S.A.* album cover. He was like, "You see how iconic this is with the bandana coming out the pocket?" The cover is extremely simple but iconic: flag stripes in the background, and Springsteen just kind of standing there like a fucking boss with his back turned.

Two or three weeks later, we shot the cover for my album. Virgil and Fabien Montique were the photographers. We did the shoot, looked at the photos, brainstormed, and then curated one of the most iconic album covers of the past ten to twenty years.

Shit, they need to hang it in the Louvre. There are two gold chains in front of an all-black background. Self-explanatory, but iconic at the same time. I couldn't have been more pleased with the way everything turned out. When I first met Virgil, *something told me* we'd create magic together. And we did. We created a lot of magic in the time we were able to work together. Man, we all miss Virgil. Super-creative dude, and a real architect. May he rest in peace.

A few years ago, I got a call from a guy named Salehe Bembury. He worked with Ye before too, but I didn't know him when they worked together. He called me because he was collaborating with Versace and wanted to work with me on the project. He was working on a shoe called Chain Reaction, and they used the same chain from my album cover as the sole of the shoe. I talked to Salehe for a few hours before I felt he was a cool dude who I wanted to work with.

Something told me he was creative and passionate about what he was trying to do. We went on to make our iconic shoe with Versace. We have a great relationship today. He's doing big things with New Balance, Crocs, and a few other brands. He's one of the people I respect creatively, and I'm thankful he reached out. I'm thankful we're still collaborating friends. He actually designed my *Rap or Go to the League* charm that I wear.

One of the things I discovered when I was trapping was that different traps had different attire. Southside niggas would be the most bummiest niggas in the world because they didn't want no attention. To this day, I got two or three homeboys that got a Bentley and only drive it for special occasions. They do the same thing with clothes. Dress like a bum unless it's their girl's birthday or something. They'll put on a nice outfit and pull out the Bentley for that. But as soon as the celebration's over, they're putting that bummy shit back on.

I remember trapping downtown in Pittsburgh, and the niggas that way had on Cartier glasses, the Deion's, all kinds of expensive designers. I would be down there looking homeless. That's how downtown Atlanta was then. Anytime somebody break into a train, or steal something from a store, the boosters would take it downtown. That's where all those guys were getting their designer stuff from. They'd get it from the boosters, put it on, and then go out. They were living life a bit more on the edge. I found myself campaigning with them a little bit more because they were driving whatever they wanted and going out more than Southside niggas.

Dolla told me once, "Man, listen. You not gone keep God-dang walking around with all this jewelry on all the time." I've been wearing jewelry my whole life. There's a picture of me from eighth grade wearing two chains, which we used for the *So Help Me God* album cover. I used to go downtown to the flea market to buy my jewelry. I was influenced by my uncle who used to have his jewelry stacked on like some Mr. T shit. Wearing jewelry was something I've always done, but my nigga Dolla told me one day, "For real Tit, you gotta take that jewelry off. You hot as a motherfucker. You can't keep walking around here like that." I would be walking into crack houses with chains on. I had to learn how not to stand out when I didn't need to.

Clubs used to be in plazas back in the day. They wouldn't be alone; they'd be attached to a Kroger or something. As a young nigga, before I could even walk into a club, I'd sit out in the parking lot and watch cars pull up. I'd watch the people walk inside.

One night a Benz pulled up and parked in front of the club. A tall bald nigga hopped out. I can almost see the car in my head. It was a white Benz coupe. I was too young to know what kind of Benz it was, but I remember the impression it left on me. Ever since that night, I've been on some wanting some more type of shit. More money, more trips, more fashion, more God, more love. I made a promise to myself to not just settle for anything.

The scene that night is still cinematic in my head. Almost like some movie-type shit. The white Benz pulled up almost in slow motion. I mean, he might've been driving slowly because the strip mall had speed bumps, but that shit still felt like a movie.

Remember how Caine pulled up to the barbecue in *Menace II Society*? He was riding slow in the 5.0 with the Daytons on it. Driving like he knew the whole damn world was watching. That's how that Benz was moving. Almost like he knew I was watching and that the moment would change me. The Benz had chrome rims, and the tires had that super-black wet shine. Man, I couldn't stop watching. The tall bald nigga gave the keys to the valet and walked into the club. He could've been a ball player, could've been a trapper. I'll never know and never saw him again.

Something inside of me did change that night though. My voice told me I could and would have everything I wanted in life. No desire was too big. No Louie designer belt too small.

XIX

HEALTH KICK

Intermitted fasting with the burpees got me looking sleek

"Life Is Beautiful"

I never really ate pork. When I was in kindergarten, my father wrote to the school and told them I was allergic to pork and not to serve it to me. My pops wasn't Muslim or Nation of Islam, but that was his way of life. My whole life I thought I was allergic to pork until one morning, after the last time my pops got out of prison, he woke me up cooking some stinking-ass bacon. I vividly remember scratching my eyes and trying to decipher the smell in my house.

"Man, what the hell is that you're cooking?" I asked him.

"Man, I found some good ole bacon," he responded. Smiling like everything was good.

"Man, what the fuck that is?"

"Bacon, man."

"You told me we don't eat no pork."

"A little pork ain't gone hurt nobody," he said, laughing.

I had to close my bedroom door and open the window. I remember that smell, it was egregious. I still laugh about that moment almost every day.

I stopped eating beef probably around my junior year in college. I was done. I used to eat Whoppers, cut in half, with all the fixings. My homie Chi, who I mentioned earlier, didn't eat beef and that just kind of trickled down to me. By then I was becoming a pescatarian, really about the seafood. This was before my rap career. When I started getting some money, I stopped going through drive-thrus. I would eat at mostly sit-down spots. That's how I would move. I stopped eating on the go. Whenever you're eating on the go, there's usually something unhealthy involved.

I feel like the music game is a sport, and what you see on the outside is a receipt of what you consume. Whatever you put in is going to get printed out at some point. You have to put the right things in to get the right things out. I'm not just talking about food but also frequencies and energies, content, music, whatever it is.

The exterior of a person is the receipt of what they're digesting. Be careful what you digest, be careful what you eat, be careful what you consume. Be conscious of what's going on around you. I tell my kids all the time when we're out, "Keep your head up, get your head out the phone. Stay in survival mode. Look around. Head on a swivel. Eyes and ears paying attention."

For me personally, I can't be sitting around eating all the wrong things and thinking I'm going to be able to move right, look good, sleep, and drip without my face being all bumpy and my energy being compromised. I take what I do for a living, my health, and my longevity very seriously. You think LeBron just be sitting around eating at McDonald's all day? Man, hell naw. That man treats his body like a temple so he can go out on the court and perform to the best of his God-given abilities. The studio, the stage, and everything associated with my career is my court. I have to make sure I'm in the best shape possible to be at my very best.

Eating all kinds of crazy shit in my forties would not support my work ethic. For years I've been working all kinds of hours, all through the night. My internal motor needs to function at a high level every day. No days off, you dig? I don't even drink sodas, but I also don't knock people who do. I've never been a moralist. I'm not perfect. I have my vices that I enjoy, but I maintain a balance with everything I do. I'm not a complete saint, but when it comes to food, I'm very cautious about what I put in my body.

One of my friends who is a serious reader and researcher put me on game. One day he broke down the chemistry of certain foods. Some of the information shocked me, and after that conversation, I was done with those foods. I can't lie though, that Wendy's ninety-nine-cent menu used to hit like crack back in the day. I remember all the burgers, the nuggets, the fries, and whatever. That used to be my shit. Folks would go crazy for that damn Frosty.

When it comes to sweets, my pops was a diabetic. So, I couldn't eat a lot of candy or a lot of sweets. I was damn near restrained from candy. That kind of got me to where I am now. I've never really been a sweets person. I remember my pops showing me how to give him insulin shots in his stomach. That was all I needed to see. My granddaddy and my uncles were diabetic. It's hereditary, so I automatically filled in that circle early in life.

I'm cool with my water and my vegetables. I definitely

like to try new foods and new vegetables, though. As long as it aligns with my dietary principles. I actually grow vegetables in my yard. I have a phenomenal garden. Everything kind of dies out in the wintertime and picks right back up in the spring. The only things I can grow in the winter are okra and peppers. I grow some banana peppers, a couple of hot peppers. I love to do that. Last season I had romaine lettuce, cherry tomatoes, cucumbers, and red and green kale. I'll go out there and grab ingredients to make me a salad. I might dress the fuck out of a turkey burger. All from my own garden.

I definitely listen to my voice when deciding what to eat. I sometimes hear it saying, *Man, it's too late to eat. You don't need to eat. You're about to lay down in the next couple of hours and have breakfast as soon as you wake up*. Or I hear it saying, *Aw man, you just had some carbs, go sweet potato instead of baked potato*. And I love baked potatoes. That right there is a struggle. Sometimes I'll get a salad and then fight with my conscience because I'll want some motherfucking fries too.

I be trying to go healthy and fried all at the same time. I'm always battling that voice in my head when it comes to eating. I'm often contemplating what I should eat first and what I should drink; when is it cool enough for me to drink some juice because I'm always drinking water. My voice always pushes me to make the right dietary choice. Just last night I was so close to ordering fries until my voice told me to go baked shrimp, sweet potato, and brussels sprouts.

My voice even shows up when it comes to my physical activity. It's my overseer: *Toni, you've been chilling way too much. Time to put some work in.* I listen because I've learned to over all the years. Some nights, I see exercises in my head, I see which exercises my body needs. I even see the order I'll do them in. Some nights my voice will wake me up out of my sleep with health instructions. *Tighten up your diet this week, tomorrow you need to do burpees, dips, and treadmill.* When I'm in my workout rhythm, boy it's something. I've always needed to incorporate working out into my life balance. That's something I want to pass on to my kids. I actually want to pass it on to all young people. Health should be a part of everything we do.

My health kick is something I like people to know about. I want people to know it's cool to eat healthy. My health kick has always been a part of my journey. Taking care of myself inside and out. I'm usually trying to balance four or five things at once: family, music, then a bunch of secondary things. I wouldn't be me if I didn't take care of my health.

Every January I hit the doctor and get a full physical. I'm talking the whole nine: cholesterol, blood pressure, sugar, you name it. I like to start off each year with that. Some of the best of us have passed on. I believe we all need to be in shape. Not like professional athlete shape, but in shape enough so that the people who depend on us can depend on us. I'm not training to be on the cover of *Sports Illustrated*. I'm going to the gym for life. I don't have a game coming up. I'm training to have longevity in the music industry. To be around a long time for my wife and kids.

Years back I had stomach issues that I needed to address. It was during a time when I was putting a lot of bullshit in my body: lean and all that. I had developed ulcers, acid reflux, and other stomach issues. I'm so happy that shit is behind me. My mom has a sensitive stomach. I think that might be hereditary too. None of my issues actually had anything to do with my diet, but I do believe my pursuit of unhealthy highs was a factor. It all ended up working for me because that scare helped me reframe my diet. I started staying away from anything that didn't agree with my stomach, especially citrus. Lemonade, oranges, all kinds of acidy shit like that. I had been abusing shit like promethazine, codeine, and paid a price. It really fucked me up.

After I got the results from the endoscopy, *something told me* it was time to switch some things up. That voice was quiet and loud at the same time. You know how they say, "That's God whispering, don't make Him yell." It reminded me that my body would break down if I didn't treat it with care.

Back in 1979, Little Richard did an interview with *Life Today* that has now gone viral. In it, he talked about how drugs started to ruin his life and why he needed to kick the habit. Something that stood out to me was when he talked about spiritual destruction and how drugs started blocking his inner voice. He said, "It wasn't no satisfaction. I was sick. I had to stay high all the time to feel like a natural person. . . . After a while, you don't hear that little voice no more." Wellness is at the core of everything. Our "little voice" is always trying to remind us. Don't get so detached that it mutes on you. I'm conscious of everything I put in my body, no matter how small. Even now, if I'm off in the club having a drink, and the bartender tries to put anything citrus in it, it's over for them. They're fired. I know that oranges are healthy, but I can't eat them. As soon as anything citrus gets into my body—five, four, three, two, one, big belch time. That's usually when I grab my stomach and call the bartender over. "Baby, are you sure this pineapple in my drink?"

XX

WORK AT NIGHT, SLEEP ON PLANES

I'm drunk and high at the same time
Drinkin' champagne on the airplane
"Mercy"

I get my best rest on planes. West Coast trips are helpful for me. When I'm in the air, I can't do anything, so I sleep great on planes. On a plane I can still text, but no matter what we're discussing, I can't do nothing until that plane hits the ground. Every time I have a flight attendant that I've had before, they tell me, "I've seen you on a flight not too long ago, but you slept the entire time." And I'm always like, "I know. You don't need to tell me."

I have rarely, if ever, overslept. It's just not in my character. Something wakes me when it's time to get up. When it's time to catch that flight, when it's time to be at one of my kids' games or events, when it's time to go get the bag. You'll never hear from me, "Aw man, I overslept, I'm sorry."

I don't need an alarm. My body will tell me mid-sleep, mid-dream, *Wrap this dream up man. It's time to get up and get our day started.* That's a part of tapping in. Are you tapped in? If not, it's time to tap in. It's time to ride. Turn the music down. Look at everything in sight. Look as far as you can. Your peripheral will cover the rest. Everything close to you. Tap in. Are you tapped in? I'm tapped in. I can feel it.

I work at night because everybody I love should be in bed asleep by a certain time. My phone isn't ringing, I don't need to help with anything. I don't need to worry about if someone ate. And I don't eat late, so I don't need to worry about eating. I can just work. I can focus on the job at hand. When I record during the day, not to say that I can't, but when I do my phone rings the whole time. It might be calls from my mom, wife, three kids, or homeboys.

Speaking of my homeboys, even them niggas are usually asleep by midnight. The night hours allow me the opportunity to focus only on what's in my control. Nighttime is when I clock a bunch of my hours in. Making music is my job. What a traditional person's nine-to-five is might be eleven-to-seven in the morning for me. I'm passionate about this here. Not all rappers or musical entertainers approach their careers like full-time jobs. Some have people who write songs for them, and they just show up when it's time to record the music. Me, I'm chopping wood every day. When I go in at night, it's the most peaceful time for me to work. I'm a little bit more unconventional. Plus, I came up under Wayne, and he raps all night.

I want to briefly talk about numbers. When people see certain numbers all the time, we can ask ourselves, "What does this mean?" "Do you know what this means?" I know that if we see the same number a bunch of times coincidentally, we might google it to find out what it means. When my wife Kesha got pregnant with Heaven, my first child, we recorded everything. We all (me, Kesha, my mom, and my pops) were damn near placing bets on when we thought Heaven would be born. I think she was supposed to be born August 10, but my mom's birthday is July 26. As you have read, me and my mama are very close. During one of the recordings, while we were guessing when Kesha would have the baby, I said loudly, "That baby gone be born the same day as my mama, watch." And just as sure, Heaven came the same day my mama came.

After Heaven, our beautiful creative kid Harmony was born. Then a few years after that, our son Halo arrived. I'll never forget the legendary stories surrounding Halo's birth. When Kesha went into labor with Halo, my mom stayed at the house in our room with Heaven and Harmony.

Halo was born around eleven-something at night on October 14. Around the time Halo was coming into the world, the alarm at the house went off, and my mom called me because she needed the password to let the security folks know that everything was fine, and we didn't need anybody to come to the house. I remember exactly how our conversation went:

"Mom, what's up?"

"Ain't nothing, I'm good." She says, "It just went off, we never did nothing. We ain't even left the room."

"Well, okay. The baby came." I remember people in the hospital room embracing.

"Oh my God, good God bless. That's such an amazing

thing. But with the alarm. I don't know what made that thing go off." The mystery of the alarm going off didn't bother me too much because I trusted my mom saying that everything was okay, and we had our new addition to celebrate.

Maybe a week later, baby Halo had been at home, and Kesha was on the computer checking her email. She ended up checking the footage from the night the alarm went off. We had motion cameras inside the house that recorded and would take a snapshot of any and all movement. Kesha ended up seeing something on the footage and called me into the room to check it out.

Man, the footage showed a vision, and we could clearly see somebody, who paused, looking as if they were walking through the house. The image was blurry, but it looked like somebody was in motion. Somebody, not really looking to bother nobody, just a curious soul walking around. We stared at the still shot closely, and the more we looked, the image became clearer. The image had a face, and it moved with a disposition I had seen before. It moved like love, like God, like an Epps. I could clearly see that the ghost was my pops.

It was written on that day of October 14, 2015. I had buried my father on July 4, 2012. I took pictures with my phone of our ghost, but anytime I would try and show people, it wouldn't show up. I sent the images to Kesha one time while we were in Florida on a boat ride. Right when I did that, it was almost like her phone crawled out of her pocket and fell into the ocean. The first thing I said was, "I just sent you the picture with Pop in it. Now your phone in the damn water." A few times, the image did show up when I tried to show people. I showed a few of my close friends and asked them, "What do you see?" They would be like, "That looks like Pops." Then I'd tell them to look at the date, and they would all get goose bumps. "Bro. That's crazy."

For some reason I don't think Pops went to the other side until we had Halo. That's probably why my son has my pops's demeanor and why he's so mature at such a young age. I later sent the ghost image to my cousin Cat, who I'm with all the time. He's like the big brother I never had. Low and behold, Pops was right there on Cat's phone. I told Cat, "You keep this because Pops is so sarcastic that when I want to show the image to people, sometimes he won't let me show it." Around that same time, I was at Ye's house, and we were talking about ghosts. I told Ye that I'd seen my father after he'd passed away. Cat was there with me. It was me, Ye, and a couple of other people I won't name.

I told Cat, "Come here, bro. Come show them that image of Pops." Cat brought his phone over to me. Right when I was ready to show Ye and everybody the picture, I knocked over a big-ass jug of lemonade. That was something I'd never done. I like to consider myself one of the coolest people on the face of this earth. I have never been a clumsy person. I said to myself, *Man, my pops is so sarcastic*. Everybody started getting up, wiping the table down. That whole chaos put the room in a different space. I don't remember if they got to see my pops. What I do know is that on the night my son was born, Pops was around. While we were bringing his grandson into the world, he was reminding us, "God is love."

EPILOGUE

THE FUCK IT VOICE

Listening to the voice in your head is all about taking a chance. It's about being confident in yourself and your lineage. It's about being confident in your connection with a higher power. You have to trust that the information coming from this voice is pure and not meant to hurt you.

I'm not saying we can't have bad voices in our head, especially if we're talking about mental illness. There's also what I call a "fuck it" voice. That's the voice that encourages you to live life spontaneously and on the edge. To not care about how your choices affect the people around you. It literally says, "Fuck it. Go ahead and do that shit."

The *fuck it* voice is loud and persuasive. That voice will have you making terrible decsions. It'll have you moving out of alignment. The *fuck it* voice is powerful and strong. It's often sporadic and feels foreign. You'll know it's not a voice with good intentions because it doesn't give you inner peace.

The righteous voice, the God voice, provides you with solitude and patience. It feels like your granny giving you a big-ass hug. I always say you have to think twice before you make a decision. That *fuck it* voice, you only think one time, and then you'll jump off the fucking roof. Have discernment. Be still. Listen carefully. Don't confuse the voices.

I've had bad voices come into my head that've told me to do some fucked-up shit. That's not God. God is love and love is God.

One time, way back when I was selling crack, I found myself in a bit of a predicament. It was the weekend, and I was doing my thing, so naturally I had crack on me. My homeboy Goat wanted to go to the club that night, which sounded right to me. We headed that way in Goat's silver Box Chevy. I can't remember which club it was, but I do remember saying "fuck it" and getting in the car with crack in my pocket. I wasn't able to put the crack away before we left, but I wasn't tripping because I knew that I'd be prepared if somebody called me for work while I was out.

We stopped at a BP gas station on the way to grab some blunts and soda, that whole thing. Left there and jumped on the ramp that led to the expressway. As soon as we got on that motherfucker, the police got behind us. I told Goat, "Aw damn dog, twelve behind us." He didn't seem to be worrying too much until I said, "Shit, boy, I got this crack on me." That's when he was like, "What the fuck do you got crack on you for? We on our way to the club. You think you finna sell some crack to somebody in the club?" I started thinking to myself, *Oh my God*. And right when I had that thought, the blue lights behind us blew up. Damn. They were pulling us over.

We pulled over, and I placed the crack in my hand. *Something told me*, "If you think fast, you can get out of this fucked-up situation." This wasn't the *fuck it* voice, it was the righteous one. There was no time to think, so I just trusted my instincts and somehow just knew what to do. The same way my mom did when she fell out in my principal's office, I went into a whole production and started acting like a paranoid passenger. I opened the car door and began exiting, unprompted.

As I was getting out, I threw the crack under the car, then stood frozen with my arms raised. "Officer, what's going on? I don't know what y'all pulled us over for." The officers yelled at me to get back in the car. I stayed in character. "I'm sorry, Officer, I just don't know what's going on. We didn't do anything," I yelled back at them and then they told me to get back in the car again, this time more forceful. When I got back in the car, Goat asked me, "Fool, what the fuck are you doing?" I saw the police walking toward the car and just stayed quiet.

When the police got to the car, they didn't even search it. That was the ironic thing about the whole situation. They asked us some questions and ended up letting us go. It was one of those rare times when that happens. We pulled away and once it felt like we were really all good, I said to Goat, "Man, I threw my shit under the car, we got to go back and get it." We ended up having to go all the way down a long stretch of the expressway to get off on the next exit. Then we had to drive back up and get back on the expressway to get back to where they pulled us over. Damn near a full circle.

But here's the crazy thing: Once we finally got back to the spot where they pulled us over, I could not find my package. It was just gone. I couldn't believe it because I knew where I'd stashed it. It didn't matter though. I shouldn't have brought it with me anyway. I listened to that *fuck it* voice and said fuck it. That almost got me locked up and fucked up.

I got a partner (I'm sure a few of us got a partner like this). He was messing around with a chick, and you know, things got heated romantically. He ended up saying fuck it and had unprotected sex with the woman. Well, she ended up getting pregnant, and he told her he didn't want the baby.

She told him, "Why did you have unprotected sex with me if now you don't want the baby?" My partner said, "I was just being sporadic in the moment and something came over me, but I don't want to have this baby." "Naw, I'm going to have this baby," she said to him.

He had no idea what to do, so he tried bribing her. That didn't work, and she had the baby. Now he hates and resents her. Got himself in a real shitty situation. At least something beautiful came out of it, a new life. I believe a baby is always a blessing. But the whole complicated, life-changing situation started with his initial fuck-it thought. That was the same voice that almost changed my life by not putting the crack away before me and Goat went to the club that weekend. That's not the voice in your head I've been talking about throughout this book.

If it doesn't involve the love part, then it can't be God. That's what this whole thing is about. It's about accepting the unknown, having faith in the unknown. Even when you're not sure that everything will work out. That's faith, right? It's about gaining enough courage to be self-aware. To move forward in your abundance, in your life, in your creativity, in your ideas at all times. That's how I've lived my life. That's what we've been talking about this whole time.

I'm someone who has defied all the odds and used this secret weapon called the voice in my head to do so. That voice has been a reference point for me, an energy to consult with, a source to share ideas with. It is the light, it is God. Can't nobody tell me no different. The voice in your head is God's whisper. It's like somebody in your classroom trying to give you the answers to a test. Life's tests. That's what it feels like to me, my energy, my life's journey, how it feels in my chakras. I'm a son of the highest power and I'm connected. Dig deep, dive inward. Accept the things you cannot change. Trust the things that feel a part of you.

Once you start tapping into your intuitive wisdom, you'll become more aware about everything. Things that come from your conscious mind and your subconscious. Ask yourself: Are your thoughts actually your thoughts or someone else's? Are they coming from social media, television, your friends, your parents, or you?

Dream awareness is an intricate part of this. Going into that dream realm knowing it comes totally from your subconscious is something to pay attention to. Remembering your dreams and taking the signs for whatever they're worth should be a part of being connected.

My granny and my aunt and them kept dream books when I was growing up. I remember my aunt would wear them old gowns. She'd wear a gown all day. She stayed with my granny for a while. My aunt was an avid antique buyer. She would go to different estate sales and yard sales and pick up different things that I'm sure now are probably worth tens of thousands of dollars. Back then, she was looked at as some type of hoarder. I will always remember seeing those dream books in my granny's house. It intrigued me growing up. I knew that I was a part of a family that had mental and spiritual range. I was part of a family that didn't stick to only traditional conventions.

Some households had *Jet* magazine, some had *Ebony*. Our households had *Eastbay* magazine (the one you'd look through for shoes you swear you're going to order but never do) and dream books. All the way down to my aunt who dipped a little snuff and played them numbers. Our households were like that. Our households were tapped in.

When your intuitive wisdom kicks in, you might set an alarm clock, but you don't need it. You wake up with a purpose. You're able to wake up knowing it's time to get up. That's part of being aware, even while you're sleep. A part of being a creative is also having that intuitive wisdom. Whether you're writing rhymes, doodling, or painting. It all comes from the same place. It all comes from a voice. If you're quiet enough and you're channeling inward, you'll be able to hear that voice loud and clear. Align yourself with yourself. Take a deep dive into the intuitive wisdom part.

The culmination of my experiences has led me to be the person I am right now. Everything I've been through leading up to this point has been a combination of my spiritual foundation, nature, and nurture. Rather it's been from outside, raised by the streets, the trap, the jungle, with the wolves. Or being shown love from my aunts, mom, cousins, and homeboys.

I'm in a place where my journey has brought me, whether up or down. I'm able to embrace and regurgitate this way of knowing because I wasn't always as close to the source as I needed to be. Having gone through my trials, I know when I'm off track. I know when I need to realign myself, and I know when I need to pray. I know how to listen to my voice and understand the importance of everything my voice or intuition is telling me. In order to tap into this unique superpower that we call intuition, you have to trust yourself. The main thing is you have to trust yourself. It's simple but it's deep. You have to trust yourself. There can be consequences when you don't listen to that voice. If your voice tells you "I don't think you should go" wherever, and you end up going, be careful. You could have a bad outcome.

Now, after reading this book, it will be no surprise to me if someone says, "You need therapy." Well, I would tell them this: This is my therapy and my navigation of choice. These philosophies and way of being are a culmination of my morals and life experiences. This writing is therapeutic for me. I'm able to hash it out and reminisce about some of the stories that remind me of how blessed I've been and how I made it here. I'm able to articulate these feelings in real time.

So, this is my therapy. As you're reading this, I'm probably on a plane right now. I might be landing soon in Las Vegas, New York, or Dubai. I might still be sleeping, having a dream about the life I've lived. The pilot might've told us to prepare for landing, but I didn't hear because I'm in high school and on my way to Starship. Once the plane starts descending, I'm probably starting to wake up, getting ready to call my loved ones and check in. This is probably around the time I thank God, when I thank you, when I thank the journey, when I thank me. Something told me to write this book.

—THE END

ACKNOWLEDGMENTS

For my mom, my rock, my queen of all queens. My heart, my twin. My refuge, my armor. My best friend. I'm a mama's boy. Tity boy. We did this journey, step-by-step. A beautiful journey might I add. Ain't no way I could imagine us having such a beautiful outcome without having a lot of income.

For my father, my other best friend. My influence. My backbone. Rest in peace. It's strange how being away from someone can actually bring you closer. You taught me how to be a leader. You taught me how to be strong. You taught me how to be confident. You taught me how to be tough. For that I'm always thankful. A lot of lessons you taught me brought me closer to not just God but to myself. It's crazy that I rediscovered your letters from prison and they read different now. They feel different, they seem different, they smell different. I can hear your voice through them. I'm still learning from some of those lessons today, more than twenty years later. Every "God is love" statement you made in each letter has allowed me to understand better what it was you meant and wanted me to let into my heart. It's been an emotional roller coaster of ups and downs.

For my wife Kesha, my day one, my ride or die, my

best friend, my lover, the mother of my kids, my angel, my support system. And my babies Heaven, Harmony, and Halo. My joy and my reason. My everything.

For my big cousins, my older cousins who helped shape me. Big Cat. The twins, Jan and Van. Rest in peace, Jan. I remember Flip and Fruit put me onto 2 Live Crew when I was a little kid. I remember thinking I was sneaking watching a flick that the twins were watching. All the good times. Kim, DJ, Kamaal, Bo, Regus, Monifah and Rashida, Rest in peace Big Ken, Mook, Char, and so many more cousins . . .

I can't forget about my homeboys, Goat and Dolla. The whole 5540 Old National shaped me. And even before that, the Jay Brown days when we used to shoot dice at his mom's house. You know, Ant Mo, Mike P., the whole crew. Dee Ace. My dog Jihad. We really apartment babies. From the Perimeter Creek, Chateau Glen, Timberlane, Cherry Hills, to the whole Southside.

So many people were a part of this. My neighbor D.C. We raised hell. Snoop. And just anybody who crossed paths with me and helped nurture this nature of mine. My management team: Street Execs. I appreciate you.

And to the book publishing crew: Derrick Harriell, my cowriter; Jan Miller, my agent; and Sir Tek, my manager. Thank you to the whole team at Black Privilege Publishing, especially: Charlamagne tha God, Libby McGuire, Melissa Milsten, Garrett McGrath, Shida Carr, Erin Kibby, and Karlyn Hixson. Everyone walked me through this process with patience and love. Y'all helped me put my story on the page the way it was supposed to sound, the way it was supposed to feel. You made sure my voice came through clear, and for that, I got nothing but respect and gratitude.

TO PUT THE MONEY
IN MY SOCK.
IT WAS TOO GOOD
TO BE TRUE.
TO MAKE THE LEFT TURN.
TO PASS ON THAT VACATION.
WOMEN ARE
BORN SUPERHEROES.
MY MOM COULD
RAISE A MAN.
MY MOM KNEW THINGS.
NOT TO TAKE ALL
THAT WEED TO SCHOOL.
MY WIFE SENSED
SOMETHING.
WOMEN ARE BORN
INTUITIVE.
A RED POLO
CAN GET YOU CAUGHT.
NOT TO TRUST THE LAW.